The Ramblings of a Woul(

A random selection of vers
and selected by me. In no [
some true stories, some ma.. up, some very
personal family stuff and some absolute
nonsense, I'll leave you to decide which is
which.
I hope you enjoy reading it as much as I did
writing it.
I won't go on about myself here as you will find
out all about me in the following pages.
As I tend to write in an East End accent, it may
help if you read in one ...

If you follow me on Facebook you may have
read most of these before but here they are in
printed form.

If you haven't seen me on Facebook, please
have a look on
Chris Ross's Pictures and Platitudes.

Well, That's about it ... Enjoy ...xx

About a Boy ...

I'd like to introduce myself, I am just a young East End Boy
Born in Mile End Hospital, Mum's little bundle of joy
I came into this troubled world in 1954
It was nine short years, of laughter and tears,
since the end of the second world war

Born into the best of times, the Sixties coming up fast
Sweeping away all our yesterdays, a new day was coming at last
But as kids in the East End of London, we didn't care about that
We played on the street and our lives were complete
with a ball and an old Cricket bat

Playing the fool, walking to and from school, because nobody then had a car
Conkers and fishing for sticklebacks, and leaving our street door ajar
Scraping our knees, saying Thank you and Please, Cream Soda and Factory gates
Learning to swear when our Mum wasn't there,
and making up games with our mates

Then came the Beatles and the Flower Pot Men,
Long hair and the short Mini skirt
I was too young to go, to San Francisco,
but wore beads and a pink paisley shirt
Suddenly the world was in glorious colour, when all had once been black and white
The Sixties went by in the blink of an eye, but the music stayed with us for life

A Mod in the early Seventies, with a Vespa and white Staypressed slacks
Sunglasses, Parka and a Ben Sherman shirt, and my favourite girl on the back
Then the pubs and the cars and the new Wimpy Bars
and drinking became all the rage
Life had moved on and some innocence gone, coinciding with my Coming of Age

The Eighties, my Thirties, my Forties the Noughties and here I am sixty years old
My Grandchildren now having kids of their own and the future as ever is Gold
I wouldn't change a day of it, through the laughter the tears and the Joy
Well, that's me introducing myself, I am just an old East End Boy

A Life of Rhyme ...

What rhymes with Orange?, What rhymes with Onions
Who'd read a poem about a Chef who had Bunions?
With all of these questions in my head all the time
I'm Living a Life of Rhyme

I once tried and failed to rhyme something with Cottage
'til I went down to Brighton and drove past Pease Pottage
I stop there for coffee now every time
I'm Living a Life of Rhyme

In the morning while yawning, I'm walking and talking
I talk to myself and find everyone gawking
I go to the pub for a Lager and Lime
I'm Living a Life of Rhyme

When I wake in my Bed words spin 'round in my head
Should I stay and turn over or get up instead ?
I go back to sleep, my brain works flextime
I'm Living a Life of Rhyme

The East End of London ...

Rows of terraced houses, three rooms up and three rooms down
Unlocked doors and hiding when the rent man came around
Cobbled streets and outside toilets, housing for the poor
The East End still bore many scars of six long years of war

Disused factories and bombed out buildings, debris round our way
To kids with runny noses, this was where we went to play
In and out of each others houses, staying out 'til dark
Round the local Cemetery that we treated like a park

Our swords were made from bits of wood, our shields of dustbin lids
We played out battles on the streets, proper warrior kids
Hop Scotch, Run-outs, Hide And Seek, a goal painted on a wall
Sunday best and Pie And Mash, swimming at York Hall

But during the 1960's, demolition was all the rage
The politicians thought we should come into the space age
So they pulled down all our houses, and built looming Tower Blocks
And for the first time in our lives, our doors had double locks

That flawed social experiment did more damage than the Blitz
They took our East End way of life and blew it all to bits
We didn't want and didn't get their "Streets up In The Sky"
But broken lifts and broken glass and no-one told us why

But typically of cockneys, we came through all that and then
They knocked down most of those monoliths and started out again
So Nazi bombs and city planners, all gave us their worst
But Eastenders are never gonna have their bubbles burst

Childhood Memories ...

Memories made in childhood, that stay with you through life
The good times and the not so good, the triumphs and the strife
The things that make us who we are, and different from the rest
The stuff of life is things that sometimes put us to the test

I don't remember much before the age of maybe eight
Playing football in the street against the factory gate
Sometimes I'd fall and graze my knee, and run indoors to Mum
That TCP swab brought a tear, but out again I'd run

A mem'ry buried somewhere, of being knocked down by a car
But nothing I could show off with, I didn't bare a scar
My first day in school uniform, I really did feel smart
The girl who sat down next to me, and stole my schoolboy heart

England won the World Cup, back in nineteen sixty six
The Beatles and The Rolling Stones and Woolworth's pick and mix
Holidays in caravans, boiled sweets and spam
Mem'ries flooding back to me that made me who I am

I remember smoking a cigarette, my mate nicked from his Dad
You should have seen the state of us, both thinking we were bad
I once bunked off from school and took a tube to Upton Park
And stood outside the West Ham ground 'til it was nearly dark

Our memories belong to us, and these are some of mine
I know that yours won't be the same, but maybe back through time
You'll recognise a thing or two, and maybe even smile
Memories made in younger days, stay longer than a while

Pie and Mash and Liquor ...

Pie and Mash and Liquor,
the nectar of the gods
Never mind your Caviar,
that's for them posh sods
Two and double, fork and spoon,
Non brewed and White Pepper
Down the market?, feelin' peckish?,
It doesn't get much better

The Cornish have their Pasties,
and of course there's Fish and Chips
The Scottish seem to like something
that they call Tatties and Neeps
But if you come from London
and if you're working class
Pie and Mash and Liquor
will be on your Epitaph

The Mash gets scraped along the plate
and the Pies put upside down
The verdant Liquor poured across
until they nearly drown
The softness of the pastry
makes this banquet taste complete
You feel like a great white hunter sometimes,
looking for the meat

But Pie and mash and Liquor,
we want it when we do
And when we do we always recommend
that you do too
But if you come from somewhere else
and it ain't in your blood
You need a taste bud transplant ...
I rest my case M'lud ....

Do's and Dont's...

We're all brought up with lists of things
We must or mustn't do
Things our Mums and Dads would say
And now we say them too
Don't walk under ladders,
And never pick your nose
Don't say what, it's pardon
As everyone now knows

Don't go out without your coat,
You're bound to catch a cold
No one likes a know it all
Or a kid who's being bold
Don't forget to clean your teeth
And wash behind your ears
Don't be rude to grown ups,
Embrace the passing years

Early to bed and early to rise,
And remember that Mother knows best
Always remember to do up your flies,
Be yourself and don't follow the rest
But the one that stuck with me through life?
It's one I'm sure you know
There's a whole lot of stuff that can make you feel rough,
...But for God's sake don't eat yellow snow ....

Mile End Boy ...

Mile End Underground station,
on the District and Central Lines
A station that, when I was young,
I always said was mine
I knew I didn't own it but it was my closest stop
I just turned right down Southern Grove
and then right at the shop

I went to Upton Park from there to watch the Hammers play
And caught an 86 outside to go to St. Paul's Way
The warm wind blowing up the stairs as the train pulled in
The sweet machine on platform two I put my sixpence in

The Odeon was opposite with the T/A next to that
The bloke there on the paper stand who wore a funny hat
The junction with Grove Road is there, just by the traffic light
We'd sit outside sayin' "Penny For The Guy"
when it came to Bonfire Night

It seemed so big, back in the day, but I guess that we were small
I went by there the other day, it isn't big at all
It's just another station on the London Underground
But not for me, a Mile End boy,
I feel I'm on home ground

He's Leaving Home ...

Now here's a little story that I've never told before
About the day that I left home in 1964
I can't remember why or what had happened way back then
But then it was so long ago and I was only ten

So off I went up Southern Grove to Mile End Road and right
And off into the big wide world ...I'd head toward the light
I didn't have a plan of course, I didn't have a clue
But I had sixpence in my pocket and a half done Scooby Doo

I'm passing by St Clements now, as a kid, a scary place
They said "It's full of nutters", so I quickened up my pace
"I'll show them", I must have thought, as I walked off that day
I'm now up by Electric House, opposite Wellington Way

As I approach the Police Station I break into a sweat
In case they have a posse out and I'm not finished yet
I run into Bow underground, to buy myself some sweets
I feel like I have walked for hours and stop to rest my feet

By now I start to wonder, why I am on the run
It's not like in the movies, it isn't that much fun
If Mum had told me off then I guess I was being bold
I wish I'd put long trousers on, my legs are getting cold

I've now passed Poplar Civic and I'm standing by Bow Church
I wonder if they're all out now and joining in the search
Maybe I should turn back now, they'd all be glad for me
And apart from any other issue, I really need a wee

....

....

I turn and smile and tell myself, they've learned their lesson well
I tread in something slippery, Oh no what is that smell?
I'm running now I must get home before it gets too late
I stop off at the bombed site for a wee, I just can't wait

My pace is now more leisurely I walk along and see
There's no-one out, they've all gone in, perhaps to have their tea
My Mum's done fish paste sandwiches, she watches me walk in
I wonder why she doesn't ask me, where the hell I've been

I've been gone nearly thirty minutes, that's really a long time
I finish off my Scooby Doo and into bed I climb
My big adventure's over, the day comes to an end
But one thing is for certain, they won't mess with me again.

School Friends ...

I went to school with Paddy Fields, a lovely Irish lad
Who always said, that when he left school,
he wanted to work with his Dad
His dad had a partner called Bernie Green,
a right old east End geezer
Whose daughter also went to our school,
and her first name was Teresa

Now Paddy Fields and Teresa Green,
they went around in a crowd
With Penny Lane and April Falls
and nobody else was allowed
They wanted to climb the social peaks,
and working on that premise
They made it their business, to befriend a lad,
in the sixth form called Ben Nevis

Well Ben's best mate was Albert Bridge,
who sat next to River Thames
River's a pretty common name now
but it wasn't way back then
Rivers girlfriend was Mary,
Mary Christmas to be perfectly clear
Like everyone else, she only saw,
her Father once a year

I often wondered, why strangers laughed,
when they saw the register at school
I wonder if it, was because the teacher,
was called Miss Molly Cule
I don't know what happened to Paddy Fields,
if he made the supreme sacrifice
But last time I heard, and it may sound absurd ...
...but I heard he was something in Rice

Rich and Famous ...

I'm gonna be really famous one day
Beyond even my wildest dreams
Don't ask me what for, 'cos I'm not really sure
But when I think of the future it seems .....

That Warhol said, that we would all have,
Our own fifteen minutes of fame
I hope when mine comes, I'm not out, 'round my Mum's
I don't think they'll deliver again

Fifteen minutes, that's not very long
To bask in the glory of fame
Really just time for a smile and a song
But at least everyone new my name

But the point is its coming and it's coming up fast
So if you want to know me, then don't be the last
'Cos all those who know me, don't worry you're in
But Johnny come latelys can whistle and spin

I'll walk down the street without missing a beat
With a hint of the Devil may care
You'll walk down the street and the people you'll meet
Will say "Ain't that Chris Ross Over there?"

I'm joking of course, I mean what would I do
With fifteen minutes of fame
You can't take it to Asda and spend it
And it goes just as quick as it came

So I'm not going to be really famous one day
But if fortune should come to my door
Before you come round to borrow a pound
I suggest that you reread verse four......

Glasses ...

Wherefore art thou now my glasses
For you are my rod and my staff
I know that you play hide and seek with me sometimes
And I know that you think its a laugh

I'm sure that I left you in the usual place
On the chest of drawers next to my bed
But I open my eyes and to my surprise
You're not there but somewhere else instead

Now I only need glasses for reading
And focusing, and seeing up close
I once sighted Venus, and you should have seen us
The night I thought I saw a ghost

But it seems that you're never around when I need you
Now, where did I leave you?..let's see
I'll tell you in verse, that I'm not sure what's worse
My eyesight or my memory

Oh there you are on the other side of the bed
How did you get over there?
I have to say you feel a bit tight on my head
That's because this is Mary's spare pair

But now I've got these on I'll find you ....
On the chest of drawers, next to my bed?
I'm sure I looked there, I think I'll get a spare pair
And sellotape them to my head .....

On The Left ...

I've been on London Transport
And I want to have a moan
Well, not just there but up in town,
I can't be on my own
This is Britain, we pass on the Left
Not on the Right hand side
I feel I want to kick against
The continental tide

Now I'm not being racist
But the rules are there for all
Not even xenophobic,
As the British also fall...
...in line when ev'rybody else
Is passing on the right
It's Left, it's Left, I scream inside
But I don't want a fight

So just like all the other sheep
I fall in with the crowd
But I swear that come the revolution,
You'll hear me singing loud
I'm walking on the wild side
And I want you to do too
But only if you want to
And have nothing else to do

We're British, we don't make a fuss,
We just let things roll on
I guess it doesn't really matter
If they get it wrong
We'll bump into each other
And say sorry, excuse me
But come on people get it right,
Or Left as the case may be

Relatives ...

I had a Nan in Stepney Green
and one who lived upstairs
I had two Uncles and two Aunts
who went around in pairs
I never had a Grandad though,
at least not one I knew
One was dead and someone said
the other one was too

But kids today have loads of them,
there's Grandad this or that
The one who moved to Spain last year
and the one who wears the hat
There's Mummy's Dad and Daddy's Dad
and Mummy's Mum's new Husband
It seems to me that kids today
have Grandad's in abundance

I guess it's got something to do with money,
we couldn't afford many rellies
A Sister, a Brother, and maybe one other,
who slept in a room at Aunt Nellie's
It's amazing what you can get these days
if you've got a couple of pound
In-laws and Outlaws, One's mine and One's yours,
there seems to be lots to go 'round ...

Productive Text ...

I've got that Productive text on my phone
and it's getting the Butter of me
It's mixing my Worms and my Letterbox up
and I ain't got my glasses to see
I wish I could Turnip this Fussing thing off
but can't Fondle the switch so I'm screwed
So whatever is showing, I'm hoping you're knowing,
what I Meander and I'm not being rude

Now, there comes a time in everyone's Loaf,
when Thongs don't go as they planned
You type the word white but it comes out as Shite,
a slip that we all understand
I have no idea, what I'm going to say
when I sit at my Lapdog to write
But with this thing turned on, and with Weirds going wrong,
this one could take me all night

So I'll cut it a little bit shorter than usual.
as the actress said to the bishop
And I'll leave you before I get into trouble
with Whirls that may get more explicit
So, If the past tense, In this didn't make sense,
the Raisin is easy to Pee
I've got that Productive text on my phone
and it's getting the Butter of me

Cheese and Onion Crisps ...

Cheese and Onion flavoured Crisps
The bestest Crisps there are
So much better than Ready Salted
Or Salt and Vin-e-gar

You can keep your Bovril flavour
And your Smokey Bacon too
And why they make Roast Chicken Crisps
I just don't know, do you?

Prawn Cocktail flavoured or Roast Beef
You can leave them where they are
'Cos Cheese and Onion flavoured Crisps
Are the bestest Crisps there are. ..xx

Gate 44 ...

Down the escalator and
along the corridor
Walk about a mile or so,
turn left and through the door
On the moving walkway
as I drag my case along
I must be nearly there by now,
did I somewhere go wrong

Final call for Ryanair
flight 205 to Dublin
Alright, alright, I say to myself,
can't they see I'm running
Up the stairs and no one cares
or gets out of my way
If I knew I had to walk this far
I'd have set off yesterday

Through the passageway
and up another escalator
I wish I'd looked, and maybe booked,
a flight that left much later
I could have walked to Dublin
by the time I reach the gate
There we are, gate 44
I knew I wasn't late...

First Kiss ...

Can I go out to play Mum,
My mates have gone over the park
They've taken a ball so they'll need me in goal
I'm sure we'll be home before dark

Yeah go on then, but mind the road
And take this threepenny bit
Get yourself something but don't spoil your dinner
We're having a nice bit of brisket

What about your brother, D'you know where he is
He went out at about half past three
I didn't let on that I knew where he'd gone
'Cos it's somewhere that he shouldn't be

He was over the debris, in the bombed houses
Smoking cigarettes and spitting and swearing
Throwing stones at the old factory windows
Getting dirt on the clothes he was wearing

So I went to the shop for some bubble gum
And got two big pennies in change
Stuffed one down each sock for safekeeping
And headed back parkwards again

When I got to the park after crossing the road
My mates were nowhere to be found
So I sat on the grass and a little girl walked past
And smiled and my world turned around

....

....

Her hair was bright blonde and in ringlets
Her blue gingham dress was too long
It had probably belonged to her older sister
And her mum had just passed it along

It was love at first sight for a seven year old
She giggled and laughed at my socks
I showed her the two bright pennies I had
And then we ran down to the shops

I bought her a bubble gum with one of my pennies
Then she kissed my cheek and I ran
All the way home, before it got dark
But I knew now that I was a man ...

Black and White Films ...

You can't beat a Black and White Movie
For me, monochrome is the best
Films that were made in the Forties and Fifties
That are still here 'cos they passed the test

Films like, "To Kill a Mockingbird",
"The Apartment" and "12 Angry Men"
It doesn't matter how often I see them
I'll always watch them again

"High Noon", "Casablanca", "Inherit the Wind"
All made in pure black and white
"It's a Wonderful Life", "Brief Encounter"
And Clark Gable's "It Happened One Night"

I know there's some great films in colour
And nothing is set in concrete
But "Passport to Pimlico" or "Kind Hearts and Coronets"
Are a wet Sunday afternoon treat

"The Man Who Shot Liberty Valance"
And "From Here To Eternity"
Or John Mills drinking Lager, in "Ice cold in Alex"
There's no need for colour for me ...

I Don't Think ...

I don't think I'll ever do that anymore
But it did seem okay at the time
Sometimes you kinda get caught in the moment
And you think it'll all work out fine

It was more of a spur of the moment thing
But then suddenly I become more alert
It's not like it's against the law or nothin'
And let's face it, no one got hurt

Choices and voices go off in our heads
And decisions, not always our own
That leave us to wonder, did I make a blunder ?
And if so, did I make it alone

I must say though it was quite funny
And I still laugh when it comes to mind
The things that we do without thinking
Lift us up or just leave us behind

It's not like there's gonna be consequences
Or that anyone will know it was me
Nothing got broken and no words were spoken
And there's no money back guarantee

It just left me wondering afterwards
Is my alibi watertight ?
I don't think I'll ever do that anymore
But then again, I just might

Born 'n Bred In London ...

Born and bred in London,
To the East of that fair town
Raised in streets of terraced houses,
Long since been pulled down
Playing football in the road,
No traffic way back then
Going In To have Our Tea,
Then Playing Out Again

We went to school in Malmesbury Road
and then to St. Paul's Way
I don't know what they're like right now
but good schools in their day
Saturday morning pictures
at The Odeon, Mile End
Pie And mash in Burdett Road
in Mrs Charles', then...
Playing on the Debris,..
Oh what fun we had
Until it's time again for bed and then
it's home to Mum and Dad

We never had much growing up,
or so our old folks say
It seemed to me we had the world
and still does to this day
Sunday morning down Brick Lane
if our Mum got us up
Tubby Isaacs seafood stall
buying cockles by the cup

....

....

"Vicky Park" on a summers day,
lying in the sun
Fishing with a hook and line,
we always had such fun

I still live in the East End now
and of course so much has changed
I love the new bits and the old,...
nothing stays the same
It's Canary Wharf or Westfield
and of course there's still West Ham
Born And Bred In London,
I guess that's who I am

Born to be a Grandad ...

Born to be a Grandad,
Never really knowing how
I made it up as I went on
And still make it up now
I love it when the girls come round,
Though one's now all grown up
She still comes round to see her Grandad
Just maybe not as much

The little ones still laugh when Grandad
Tells a joke or farts
It's like a little sitcom in
Which they all play their parts
I never know who has more fun
When we play silly games
And make up songs that usually end with
Monkeys with their names

Their laughter is infectious
And I can't help but join in
We build sandcastles, feed the ducks
And empty the biscuit tin
The card tricks and the shadow puppets
And Movie night allow
Me to be a Grandad,
Never really knowing how

As Usual ...

It's all very quiet in our house tonight
As usual when the Kids have gone home
It looks like a war zone in our house tonight
As usual when the Kids have gone home

We'll put away ev'rything that came out to play
Find all the things where they've tucked them away
Change the Bed Clothes for next time they stay
As usual when the Kids have gone home

Soon we'll welcome the quiet and peace
Our feelings of sadness as always decrease
Wishing they were here will very soon cease
As usual when the Kids have gone home

I miss them already as ever I do
It's lovely when they say that they'll miss me too
I'm planning the next time and what we will do
As usual when the Kids have gone home

I'm still smiling now at some things that they said
"In your face Grandad" and "Carry me to bed"
I'll have to carry Mary upstairs instead
As usual when the Kids have gone home

Change the World ...

If no one would do what you wouldn't do
For all the tea in China
And you wouldn't do what they wouldn't do
Then who's gonna be the designer?

Who's gonna say, there must be a way
That's different from what we do now
No one would try and no one would fly
Nothing would change anyhow

The point I am making, is get up and do it
Go forth and stand out from the crowd
Don't be constrained by what others have claimed
Is too weird and should not be allowed

Now before you go out there, and tear up the rule book
Just make sure that no one gets hurt
Don't try changing all things, just start with the small things
Not everyone wants to convert

I'm starting today but not in a big way
I'm wearing odd socks for a change
And maybe I'll wear my new underwear, back to front
Although that would be strange

Smile at a stranger, avoiding the danger
Of getting involved in a chat
Good Morning will do, and if said back to you
Then at least you'll know that you did that

So enjoy your day and I'll have to say
Don't do anything I wouldn't do ...
Though maybe you should, because I know I would
But then only if I was you ....

A Message To Youth...

We didn't look like this when we were younger
We didn't suffer daily aches and pains
We didn't wear too many clothes in summer
Or carry an umbrella in case it rains

We didn't always stop for no good reason
Or walk as slowly as we seem to now
We didn't always talk about the weather
Or moan because the music is too loud

We didn't always holiday in winter
Or stay in and watch T.V. on New Years Eve
We never thought the world had gone to hell in someone's handbag
That's something passing years have us believe

You still don't know the value of a lovely cup of tea
In a little seaside café in the rain
Or to stop and take a seat and chat people that you meet
Or to travel 'cross the country in a train

The beauty of a sunrise or a picnic on the beach
Watching Casablanca once again
Knowing things like, Cary Grant's real name was Archie Leach
Or singing all the words to Penny Lane

To watch the Antiques Roadshow and to doze off in your chair
And to reminisce with friends of glory days
To drive past your old school and be delighted it's still there
Or to sit and watch your grandchild while she plays

Youth is wasted on the young or so old people say
And also that you reap just what you sew
If you're lucky you'll turn out the same as us one day
It's great here and I thought you'd like to know ....

Mother's Day ...

I just want to say Happy Mother's Day
To the best Mum that I ever had
Well, the only one to be perfectly honest
A fact of which I am quite glad

Can you Imagine having two Mums?
To lick their hankie and then wipe your face
To put TCP on a scratch on your leg
Or to enter the Mum and Son race

Two Mums to make you eat Brussels
And two Mum's to send you to bed
Two Mums to tell you, you're not watching Tele.
You're doing your homework instead

Two Mum's to take you to the doctor
Two Mums to kiss you goodnight
Two Mum's to tell you you're her little soldier
And to make everything be alright

No, if you're like me then I'm sure you'll agree
That the truth is when all's said and done
One Mum will do and I'm glad I got you
I love you, Happy Mother's Day Mum ...xx

Father's Day ...

I know that my Dad wasn't Superman
I know that he didn't know it all
I know that he didn't always do the right thing
And sometimes he made the wrong call

I'm not going to exaggerate his virtues
Or make him to sound like a saint
Or transform his life into some fabled tale
That would make my life something it ain't

But all that been said, yes I loved him
And wish that I still had him here
We'd laugh and we'd sing and tell a few jokes
And go to the pub for a beer

He was a great teller of stories
And sure had a good few to tell
The stories got better, each time he told them
And his part in them grew as well

Now talking of singing, he had a great voice
Something to which I aspire
We once sung together, on stage in a pub
And satisfied my heart's desire

Now some people say we were peas in a pod
And I guess in someways we're the same
I see him sometimes, in the mirror when I shave
But I know it's my age that's to blame

I still smile when I think about him
And some of the things that we've done
I love you Dad, and I miss you too
Happy Fathers Day... Your Loving Son.

Bad Dreams ...

As I was cleaning my windows today,
and looking through the glass
I saw some people who weren't there
and smiled as they walked past
I don't know if they saw me
but they waved a big hello
When I turned 'round, they were still there,
I didn't see them go

The Man walked upright with a stoop
and only had one ear
Although I couldn't see his left hand side,
there could have been one there
His wife was an extremely tall woman
somewhere around four feet ten
I didn't notice her hair colour at first
and then didn't notice again

It was good to see them both again
as I'd never seen them before
I was ever so happy they didn't come,
and knock on my street door
So when I went to answer it,
imagine my surprise
The phone wasn't ringing after all,
someone was telling me lies

So anyway back to the windows
and a bucket of wallpaper paste
While Mary Berry, was baking a cake,
and asked if I wanted a taste
As we head down to Brighton to play on the sand,
and end up in Margate instead
I knew that I shouldn't eat pizza tonight,
just before I went to bed

Come Dance With Me ...

The averts in the windows down in Soho tell their tale
Of loneliness and desperation and short term love for sale
The business cards in phone boxes, more graphic by the day
I guess for some girls sometimes, they can see no other way

But I remember, long ago, I saw one on a wall
It simply said " Come Dance With Me" and really that was all
A telephone number, and a picture, of some Ballet shoes
And I still wonder, to this day, why would someone choose...

...to advertise themselves this way and who would take a chance
Or do I do this lady wrong? and did she want to dance?..
Either way the sadness of it, haunts me to this day
I hope she found someone to dance, or found another way....

A Day Out ...

It seems the sun's forgotten that it's August
Or maybe just forgotten where I am
But in the parlance, of the movies, in a gentler time
Frankly Scarlett, I don't give a damn

The wife and I are heading down to Brighton
For a walk along the prom and Fish and Chips
And to find that sweetie shop where we always seem to stop
For some Cola Cubes and a quarter of Sherbert pips

We'll talk of life in general and we'll window shop and dream
And if the sun should find us maybe sample some ice cream
Drive back along the coastal route and out past Beachy Head
Pevensy Bay, Bexhill on Sea and Hastings or Battle instead

I hope you have a lovely day and before this Sunday's done
You've eaten, drunk and rested but above all had some fun
We'd love to take you with us but we don't know where you are
Above all that, I don't think that, you'd all fit in our car

An Age Thing ...

Now, I don't know if this is an age thing
'Cos i don't know when was the first time
But you know when you wake up in the morning
And you can't seem to make the world rhyme

You know that it must be the morning
Because outside the darkness has gone
And you know that it must be a weekday
'Cos the Alarm clock radio's come on

But your mind can't put these things together
So you lay there and think for a while
Then something clicks and then it all sticks
....together and you raise a smile

Now you're not sure why you're smiling
Good Lord "Am I losing my mind"
So you leap out of bed, with a song in your head
And look out of the window to find ..

That the new day has started without you
Now what kind of day will it be
Now here's the thing, Is it Winter or Spring?
It's an age thing, or it could just be Me .....

First Car ...

My first car was a Morris Minor
An old split windscreen job
My step-dad picked it up from someone
Who owed him a couple of bob

It had a side valve engine
Which we soon took out and dumped
And replaced it with a 100cc..
...reconditioned lump

The indicators popped out the side
In a nineteen fifties style
We replaced them with the blinking ones
Though the old ones made me smile

I stuck a tax disc on the window
And doubled it's value right there
The headlining was long since gone
But I really didn't care

The car was black, the seats were red
The tyres were mostly bald
The rain came in and soaked the mats
Sometimes the engine stalled

My mates all wanted flasher cars
And I know how that feels
But here I was, at seventeen
And I had my own wheels

....

....

That old car took me ev'rywhere
And never gave me strife
It became a real big part of me
And opened up my life

I can't remember what happened to it
Or how it met it's end
I guess it just gave up the ghost
And never ran again

The old car gone and I moved on
And time has done it's worst
It doesn't matter what you drive
You don't forget your first

Penny Wise ...

So, Mr and Mrs Albert Wise
had a daughter they called Penelope
Never thinking, that of course one day,
her name would be shortened to Penny
Penny Wise, I ask you... there's a name to take through life
She couldn't wait for the day to come,
when she was somebody's wife

Old folk would ask, are you Penny Wise ? ...
and are you Pound Foolish as well?
They all thought that they were the first with that joke,
by their big silly grins you could tell
She just didn't think it was funny,
the humour went over her head
She'd never even heard the expression,
but she smiled every time it was said

Now, Penny had boyfriends a plenty,
Jimmy Farthing and Jonathan Chew,
William Change and the unusually named
Joe Arcade to name but a few
She couldn't marry any of these,
even if she thought she might
She just couldn't handle, being with Simon Candle,
that time that he asked for a light

But one day she met him, the man of her dreams,
It really was love at first sight
She never enquired about his surname at first,
somehow it didn't seem right
He asked for her hand and it went as he planned,
He'd be Tarzan and She would be Jane
Dearly beloved, we're gathered together to join .....
Penny Wise and Mike Lane ....

The Bike Shop ...

She worked in a Bicycle Hire shop in Brighton
He wanted to ask for a date
She lived in a bedsit in a big Georgian house,
He shared a flat with his mate

It was love at first sight and he dreamt that he might
One day walk with her down the church aisle..
He'd too caught her eye but like him she was shy,
This whole thing could take quite a while

He rented a bike every weekend
Just to go into the shop
She never caught on, it was her all along
But she just hoped that he'd never stop

It would have been cheaper to buy one
She thought as she served him again
And why is he renting a Bike on a day
When it's quite clearly going to rain

She asked, Are you off somewhere special
As his helmet slipped over his head
He didn't ignore her, he only lived for her
He just didn't hear what she said

Then came the day he decided,
He would ask her, what had he to lose
He'd put on his favourite tee shirt
And even wiped over his shoes

She said what can I do for you this fine day
He said, walk with me 'til it's dark
She works in a Bicycle Hire shop in Brighton
While he takes their kids to the park

Facebook Addict ...

My name is Chris I am an addict
Facebook is my drug of choice
I used to keep all of this crap in my head
But now find that I have a voice

I now share my thoughts with the planet
Not that the world really listens
I know that you've heard, you can't polish a turd
But trust me, sometimes this stuff glistens

I'll carry on posting my pictures
And poems and musings on life
I'll get your reactions and once in a while
Remember to talk to my wife

I can't stand not being connected
I hate it when I am off-line
I switch on my phone, the 3G kicks on
A cup of tea, and I'm just fine

When people come 'round here to visit
I still keep my hand on my mouse
Thank God I've got WiFi and work off a laptop
I can go anywhere in the house

I know that one day I will stop this
A sentence that's often been heard
I'll go back and find, the life I left behind
If I can remember the Password

Early Television ...

I remember watching Danger Man,
The Saint and Captain Scarlett
And also The Avengers, when Honor Blackman was a starlet
Armchair Theatre, Robin Hood
and Fireball XL5
The Champions, All Gas and Gaiters
and of course This is your Life

Father Dear Father, Man in a Suitcase,
Randall and Hopkirk Deceased
Dickie Henderson, Double Your Money
and Till Death Us Do Part was released
Mrs Thursday, Doctor Finlay, Harry Secombe and Friends
Morcambe and Wise, Coronation Street,
Please Sir and Emergency Ward Ten

We only had two channels then or three if your family was rich
BBC2 was still pretty new but everyone wanted to switch
Then someone would knock the aerial over and,
that's it, the picture was gone
So you'd twist it and turn it, "Is that any better" ?.
"Hurry up 'cos Wagon Train's on"

All this on a screen, the size of an Ipad,
on a Telly. as big as a car
Technology moved on, and those days are gone,
It's amazing that we've come this far
But with Fifty Inch Plasma and HD and Colour,
and a picture that looks like it should
Hundreds of channels and LCD panels,
The programmes just don't seem as good ....

Dance ...

I had a thought this morning, while laying in my bed
Get up you Lazy Sod I thought... but I lay there instead
Listening to the Poni Tails, singing "Born too late"
Born too late, but Awake too soon, the clock said 6.08

I had to shave and shower, just as I do ev'ry day
Then sit and write a quick hello before I'm on my way
So I put one leg, out of bed, and they played "Little town Flirt"
I pulled my leg back into the bed, another three minutes won't hurt

I love the sixties music and don't hear it near enough
Three in a row and what do you know they played "To Sir With Love"
What a voice that Lulu had and what a Mighty song
I could lay in bed and listen to this music all day long

But I know, I have places to go, and people that I have to meet
So up I get, with a spring in my step, the music had got to my feet
I mention this to say to you that if you get the chance
Play some music for yourself that makes you want to dance

Moonwalk down the corridor and tap dance in the lift
Shuffle round the office with a little sideways drift
Do it though, so no one knows, It's funnier that way
It also stops the Men in white coats, Coming to take you away...

The Flight Home ...

I'm watching the guy sat in front of me
As his ears seem to flap back and forth
I think that he's having the Chicken for dinner
And he's chewing for all that he's worth

It looks like it may be a little bit tough
The way that he's chewing that thing
I'm glad that before we got on to the plane
We popped back into Burger King

By the time you read this we'll have landed
When I can get back on the net
I've been off-line now for nearly an hour
And can feel my palms starting to sweat

Well, only a couple more hours
And we'll be back in London again
I might get a quick Chinese takeaway later
To remind us of our time in Spain

We've been through the gamut of weather
From glorious sunshine to rain
But all that and aeroplane food won't stop us
And I'm sure we'll soon go back again..

Cliché...

It's always darkest before the Dawn
Kids today, don't know they're born
It's better to have loved and lost
Know the value, Not the cost

Never test a battery, with the tip of your tongue
When you carry scissors, always walk don't run
Never play with fire or you know that you'll get burned
And of course A penny saved is like another penny earned

Words of wisdom, we all knew
Our parents taught us as we grew
But do they stand you in good stead
They ought to they're still in your head

Do unto others as you would be done to
A stitch in time saves nine
Never change horses in midstream...
Always a favourite of mine

Not that I ever rode a horse
A bike was my trusted steed
But I never changed it or rode in a stream
Only through a puddle at top speed

....

....

Stand your ground and face your fears
Always wash behind your ears
Variety is the spice of life
But covet not your neighbours wife

Money, doesn't grow on trees
Remember your Thank Yous and always say please
If the wind changes, you'll stay like that
Please put a penny in the old man's hat

Teach your children what your parents said then
Life doesn't change much, it's us
Respect older people, because I'm one of them
I'll leave it with you ...... Discuss

The Wedding ...

Everyone we knew was there, our friends and family too
They'd come that late September day to hear us say I do
The slate grey steeple of the church, against the clear blue sky
No single cloud appeared that day, they didn't dare to try

I stood there at the altar with my brother, my best man
Waiting for your entrance and the chance to take your hand
Then the music started, we all knew "Here Comes The Bride"
I turned around and saw you and my heart just swelled with pride

I couldn't take my eyes off you as you walked down the aisle
Your dad there walking slowly with you, I couldn't help but smile
The sight of you in that white dress, and veil, you looked so young
I knew then I'd take care of you until our time was done

The priest said "We are gathered here...the place fell in a hush
We sang the songs we'd chosen and I swear I saw you blush
When we left there, hand in hand, they called us "Man And Wife"
The start of our adventure that we call our married life

We danced to "Whoops Upside Your Head" our wedding song was strange
You ripped your dress in the conga line, and had to go and change
We stayed 'til last, we didn't want to miss a single thing
Of that day when you answered yes and chose to wear my ring

I loved you then, I love you now, the years have rushed away
We've got a little older but I still think of that day
The story that we started on the day we joined as one
Has been a roller coaster ride ... I knew you were the one

3.23 ...

It's pitch dark at 3.23 in the morning,
I'm sure you won't be surprised
But that's the time that I keep waking up,
the time that I open my eyes
Could there be magical forces afoot ?
Could the spirit world come into play?
It's more likely some inconsiderate git,
beginning or ending their day

Now I like the mornings, and watching the Sunrise
it's my favourite time of the day
But 3.23? are you joking with me? there has to be some other way
I need to investigate what's going on because
Why, is what I need to know
I need the the services of Jessica Fletcher,
or even Hercule Poirot

Maybe I'll do the research myself,
I'm sure that would be much more fun
I could speak in a fake Belgian accent
and discover the warm smoking gun
Or look startled at being a middle aged woman
who just wrote a best selling book
Who finds all the clues. puts them together
and invites the policeman to look

Or maybe Lieutenant Columbo would say,
"I'm sorry, there's just one more thing"
Or Kojak would say "Who loves ya Baby"
but please, never ask him to sing
No I have a better idea than all that,
I know now what I'm going to do
They will not wake me, at 3.23,
I'll set my clock for 3.22....

With an E...

Born in Mile End hospital, in Bancroft Road E1
An early Christmas present wrapped and handed back to Mum
December 1954, a fair old time ago
Then taken home to Salmen Street, off Southern Grove in Bow

And so began my early life, a child of the East End
They call us Baby Boomers now, we didn't know that then
Rows of terraced houses, built to hold each other up
A pub on every corner, and West Ham won the cup

Pie and mash and Vicky park, my old man's a dustman
Hackney marshes, national health glasses
and Saturdays down The Roman
Swimming at the Muni and Sundays down the lane
Given the chance I know in advance I'd do it all again

I'm proud to come from where I do and proud of who I am
From East End Boy through woe and joy and now to East End Man
I never strayed too far away It made no sense to me
If your gonna live in London, have a postcode with an E

West Ham Fan ...

Does anyone remember, back in 1964
When West Ham won the F.A.Cup,
led out by Bobby Moore
Johnnie Sissons, Ronnie Boyce
and Geoff Hurst hit the net
It finished up 3 - 2 to us,
but took some toil and sweat

The boys came down the Mile End Road
In an open top claret and blue bus
We cheered and clapped as they went by
And they waved back at us
And then the European Cup Winners Cup In 1965
We won 2 - 0 against the Germans
It felt good to be alive

Then came 1966, and it was England's year
World Cup Willie, red white and blue,
was all that you would hear
England played their football
In a kind of West Ham mode
And we all know, The Jules Rimet,
Belonged in Barking Road

That really was the heyday
For the boys at Upton Park
We pray one day those times come back
To lead us from the dark
We're moving soon to The Olympic Stadium,
Maybe then we can......
But it doesn't really matter,
I'll always be a West Ham fan

Act Your Age ...

I know I'm getting older
but I'm only fifty eight
I don't feel like I'm ready yet
to stand by Heaven's gate
But tell me this, just so I know
that we're on the same page
What pray, are the virtues of,
and how to act your age

Do I stop saying "Tune" when I hear my favourite song
Do I stop wearing Tee shirts with designer logos on?
Are jeans and trainers now to be a thing of yesteryear?
Are Next and Fat Face, Gant and Gap just places I should fear?

No, I'll sing along to ev'ry song,
just like I've always done
I'll wear my boot cut jeans and
Beatles tee shirt in the sun
I'll listen to Sinatra,
then play some Eminem
I'll play guitar and sing the songs
of Willie Nelson then

So, not for me the casual wear
of Marks And Spencer yet
Nor any clothes sent to my house
when purchased on the Net
I'll Moonwalk while in Westfield
if the Grandchildren are there
I know they get embarrassed,
but I really never care

Now I'll say this to, any Youth who thinks,
That I have passed my prime
I've been your age, and I moved on
And you've yet to be mine.

Two ...

I wonder if you've thought that much,
about the number two ?
And how many times you use it
in most everything you do
I'm talking about a number
and the massive role it plays
In everybody's daily lives
and in so many ways

Two arms, Two legs, Two soft boiled eggs,
Two sugars in your tea
Two pies and mash for a spot of lunch,
now that's a bit of Me
Two wheels on a bicycle,
it takes Two for one to be wrong
Torn between Two lovers in a 1970's song

There are Two sides to every story
and at least Two stories to tell
Two horsemen of the Apocalypse,
and another Two as well
What once was Two for the price of one
is Buy one get one free
And we know Sylvester Stallone should have stopped,
at one film before Rocky 3

Two eyes, Two feet, Two hands to greet,
Two thumbs to show belief
And all I want for Christmas, is my Two front teeth
Two to Tango, Two of a kind, Two to make You and Me
All that I'm saying is with this inflation
you'd think one of them would be Three ....

Puddles ...

The puddles on the ground reflect the colour of the sky
The slate grey hue, reflects the mood, of people passing by
Umbrellas up, and run for cover, here it comes again
Our joint demeanour, seems to be, determined by the rain

A car goes by and splashes you, your feet are now wet through
You start to wonder just what else this day can throw at you
You should have phoned in sick and spent the day at home in bed
Or at the very least, taken the Underground instead

And then the sound of children's laughter, as they splash and play
Their oversized Sou'westers match the macs they wore today
Their brightly coloured Wellingtons that keep their feet bone dry
Jumping in the puddles, and you know you'd like to try

They are the only splash of colour, that you've seen all day
Their sense of fun and joyous screams, will chase the clouds away
So just because it's raining, don't let the weather drive you wild
Buy a pair of Yellow Wellies... release your inner child

Turned into Me ...

If when you woke from your slumber today
You laid there a little too long
Listening to the alarm clock radio
Playing your favourite song

If you had to go straight into the bathroom
To shower and do bathroom stuff
And find that your wife has put the new towels out
And your face is covered in fluff

If you then came downstairs to decide what to wear
And what you wanted was on the clothes horse
So you went back upstairs to decide what to wear
But nothing else fits right of course

If you sat down and turned on your laptop
And wrote a nonsensical rhyme
Then looked at clock as you put on your sock
And found out you'd run out of time

Knew you'd be late to pick up your mate
And you didn't have time for your tea
You'd better take fright because overnight
You've all gone and turned into me

Falling Asleep ...

The more the years pass by me
And the more of life I reap
One of life's great pleasures now
Is dropping off to sleep

I don't mean going up to bed
And sleeping through the night
Although that's very nice indeed
It's the catnaps that I like

You know when you're watching the Telly.
And your eyelids begin to close
You reach a semi consciousness
And then you start to doze

That's the bit I love the most
The bit there in between
Not asleep but not awake
As you slip into a dream

I only need five minutes
And then I feel better by far
Falling asleep is the best thing there is
But don't do it driving the car ...xx

The Dentist ...

So there I am, sitting in the dentist chair
"Open wide and let me have a look in there"
Upper right Occlusal .. left three Buccal,
Distal, Amalgam, Crown and Enamel

With all his fingers in my mouth
And a mirror a pick and some suction
He chooses now as an appropriate time
To start a conversation

Where are you going for your holiday?
He asks with genuine interest
Mwhh ooorrr llaaauueer I say
I think he must have guessed

"Oh, I've been there, you'll love it"
He answers with a straight face
Have you ever been there before?
Haww herer harrer hace !

Then the pretty Nurse appears
And joins in with our chat
Would you like to have a rinse ?
Hoow Hee hee Haww harat ..

But now the ordeal's over and my mouth again is clear
That's me done with dentists for at least another year
How much do I owe you I ask him with my usual fear and dread
Haah her hooherryharansa ... I think that's what he said ....

People ...

I've just come back off holiday
And I've come to one conclusion
And I'm gonna tell you the truth of it,
Just to save any confusion

People get on my flipping nerves
And I'd much rather be on my own
I'll tell you for why, well at least I will try,
If you'll listen while I have a moan

People on aeroplanes who talk too loud
And lay their seats back just because they're allowed
People with kids who just let them scream
And then think it's funny, d'you know what I mean?

People who insist that you hear what they think
And while we're on it, people who drink
People on bikes and people in cars,
People in shops and people in bars

People who whisper, people who shout
Tall people, short people, skinny or stout
People on Telly. In reality shows
Don't start me on them, they get right up my nose

People who clap when the aeroplane lands
People who have too much time on their hands
People who write prose, to leave us in no doubt
Oh yeah, that's Me, we'll just leave that one out

....

....

People who sit next to me, on the beach,
So flipping close that they're almost in reach
Strangers who talk to me in a queue
I flippin hate people, honest I do

Except for my family, I love them of course
And obviously my friends, they've become my life force
The people on Facebook and my old pals from school
And the People I worked with, I still love them all

I quite like the guys that I meet at the Golf course
And the girls in the coffee shop too
So, apart from these minor exceptions
I guess that just leaves Me and You ...

And you're my favourite ...xx

New Glasses ...

I'm up in town again today,
it's for an eyesight test
I keep on bumping into things
so it's probably for the best
I've popped in for a coffee
in a coffee shop I know
I've got a half an hour to spare
where did you think I'd go ?

Now I would have gone to Costa
'cos they brew my favourite cup
But when I got to the one in Cheapside
the place was all full up
So for a change I've gone round the corner
and into Starbucks instead
When I look out the window the dome of St. Paul's
and a bald eagle looms overhead

Well, I think it's an eagle, it's not very clear,
the windows are a little steamed up
And maybe that parrot that's eating a carrot
is just steam rising up from my cup
But down in the square I just stop and stare
as a cop on an elephant passes
It wasn't of course it was just a grey horse
You're right I do need new glasses

Happy Days ...xx

30th Anniversary ...

Today is our very special day,
Our anniversary
We've been married thirty years,
young Mary Coyne and me
All those doubters, years ago
who said it wouldn't last
Yet thirty years have been and gone
and been and gone so fast

We've been married for thirty years
for better and for worse
For richer for poorer, in sickness and health,
and loving for all we were worth
Through ups and downs, through smiles and frowns,
through laughter and a few tears
She's put up with me, I've put up with her,
for thirty glorious years

We may as well go the distance now
As if there was even a choice
Step by step , joined at the hip
Three Decades, Two Hearts, One Voice....

Our Baby's Having a Baby ...

I remember when she was a baby,
a Red Headed bundle of joy
She used to come round to her Grandad's for the weekend,
and I was her favourite boy
She has a new favourite boy these days,
and another one soon on his way
But I know I still hold a place in her heart,
and she's there in mine everyday

Yes, our Baby is having a Baby,
our little one's gone and grown up
Her Blanket and Bottle have had to give way,
to her own baby's Christening cup

I remember our nights out at Pizza Hut,
and the Chicken wings and Salad she had
With an extra spoonful of Bacon Bits,
that she used to get for Grandad

The memories we made are forever,
with Missy and Mary and Me
And Barney, the purple dinosaur,
and days down at Southend on sea

Polly, Paige and Jessica,
were the friends that she had at school
She told us so many stories of them,
we felt just like we knew them all

And now for the next generation,
I know that she'll be a great Mum
And I'm gonna be a Great Grandad
and plan to be part of the fun
Robyn, we love you as much as ever,
and John and the new baby too
I'm proud as a peacock to be your Grandad,
but mostly I'm so proud of you ...xx

Another Flight Home ...

A thousand miles from home and seven miles up in the sky
Crammed inside a Baked Bean can, the only way to fly?
Squashed into a seat that wouldn't suit a ten year old
The air conditioning's set too high, your left side's getting cold

We trust our lives to "I'm Ted Baker, I'll be your pilot today"
We've never seen or met this guy, perhaps it's better that way
But shouldn't Ted be designing stuff to sell in all his shops?
Perhaps it's a different Ted Baker, and then the air-con stops

It's getting hot in here and someone's taken off their shoes
Or could that be the Cheese Roll lunch? the only answer's booze!
But the car's parked at the airport and I shouldn't drink and drive
So maybe I'll just shut my eyes, and sleep 'till we arrive

I'm woken by a screaming kid, "Ah bless him", says his dad
That's not what I was thinking but there's no sense getting mad
The seatbelt signs go on and then the landing gear comes down
It won't be very long before we're down there on the ground

We'll get our bags, from the carousel, they'll probably come off last
Then stroll through customs, nonchalant, and when that hurdle's passed
Through one more barrier, round the bend and now the end's in sight
But all in all, I have to say... That wasn't a bad flight.

Old Friends ...

We share the odd glass just to help the time pass
As we speak of our wishes and dreams
We talk of the past and how time goes so fast
And how life seems to mock all our schemes

Of laughter and tears, of comfort and fears
Shared memories of life's dividends
Triumph and disaster, Love ever after
And the pure joy of being Old Friends

Mem'ries of nights of the Razzle
Of Wine and of Women and Song
Things we'll remember forever and ever
Most of them probably wrong

Do you remember, that time one December
When we did this that or the other?
I'm sure that you do, I'm sure it was you
Or perhaps it was me and your brother

Our recall may fade as the years pass away
And maybe the drink plays it's part
We laugh even more at the fact we're not sure
But the memory gives way to the heart ...

The Henley Regatta ...

There's something frightfully British
About going to Henley on Thames
Sitting and eating an egg and cress sandwich
And sipping a cold glass of Pimms

Men in Striped blazers and panama hats
Ladies in long summer dresses and flats
Rowers and Punters all drift down the river
All somehow in ways just the British deliver

Hello, how are you?...my what a nice day
Your hat is a corker sir, I have to say
Could you please tell me the way to the loos?
Are we allowed in the bar without shoes?

Laughing too loud as the rich often do
Strawberries and cream and a nice tall gin too
Deckchairs and blankets all strewn on the grass
Waving and cheering at the boats as they pass

Music and dancing or a nice gentle snooze
Too much too eat and then far too much booze
The racing and gazing at the classes who chatter
A wonderful day at the Henley Regatta

Great Grandad ...

Today I became a Great Grandad
The circle of life takes a turn
A young Man steps up to the table
A lesson in life we'll all learn

Our lives have been changed in an instant
There's one more to love and to cherish
Ten tiny fingers and Ten tiny toes
And hair that's a little...Well, Reddish

So to Robyn, our beautiful grandaughter
And to John who's the man that she chose
Thanks for those ten tiny fingers
And thanks for those ten tiny toes

For Johnny ...

I hope you splash in puddles
and your socks and feet get wet
I hope you run and chase a ball
you're never going to get
I hope you ride your bicycle
'til your legs begin to ache
And climb a tree for conkers,
or just for climbings sake

And if you fall when climbing,
and if you scrape your knee
If Mummy or Daddy aren't around,
I hope you run to me
I hope your childhood's one that's filled
with happiness and joy
And that you'll help remind me,
what it's like to be a boy

I hope you'll come to my house
and maybe stay the night
I hope you'll call my name out
if the dark gives you a fright
I hope you'll love your Great Grandad,
as much as I'll love you
I hope I haven't hoped too many things
for you to do

I hope you learn to smile a lot
just like your Mummy does
And play your football, like your Dad,
and never make a fuss
I hope one day I'll get to teach you
how to play Guitar
But most of all I'm here to help you,
be the boy you are

Braces ...

I wish that braces would come back in fashion
I'm remembering how comfortable it felt
To have your trousers held up by your shoulders
And to never have the need for a belt

I'd also fancy, higher waisted trousers
That fitted, "Larger Gentlemen" with ease
With pocket space to fit you phone and wallet
And your reading glasses, handkerchief and keys

I hate it when your trousers go under your belly
Which, let's be honest, most of us now have
It makes your shirt look scruffy and it makes your tie too short
And your belt looks like it's cutting you in half

I want a suit that fit's me, and not one I have to fit
And no one sells a Double Breasted jacket
A nice grey pinstripe, like I wore in 1986
I'd need to find a tailor who could make it

And that would be my Suit for all occasions
Weddings, Funerals and my Sunday best
But Marks and Spencer, Selfridge's and even House of Frazer
Just sell those young boy's suits, like all the rest

"Slim Fit" suits don't fit those who are not so slim or fit
But a well cut Double Breasted would be smashing
Surely I'm not on my own when I have this little moan?
I wish that braces would come back in fashion

English ...

English by the grace of God,
part of every rock and sod
Each blade of grass each grain of sand,
that make this Green and Pleasant land
Strong of spirit, fair of mind,
Pride and Passion intertwined
English by the grace of God,
part of every rock and sod

Moors and gorse and Mountain reaches,
Tree lined streets and Sandy beaches,
Fish and Chips and Dragon slaying,
A cup of Tea and England playing,
Our Mother tongue so widely spoken,
even if sometimes it's broken
English by the grace of God,
part of every rock and sod

Village Greens and Cricket balls,
Run down Barns and Marbled Halls
Pubs and Churches, side by side,
Picnics by a Riverside
Shakespeare, Churchill, Bobby Moore,
Drake and Nelson and so many more
English by the grace of God,
part of every rock and sod

You're Gone ...

I woke up this morning
And there you were gone
I just don't know what I'll do now,
You've been a big part of my life for so long
Now I must live without you somehow

I took you for granted for such a long time
but you'd have to admit you were slow,
Sometimes I'd complain
when it wasn't the same
But I just never thought you would go

So I'll have to change, and do something else
In the Mornings but on reflection,
It's not the end of the world ...There you are
You're back........
Flippin' internet connection

Manners ...

I'm not going to walk on the left anymore
I'm not going to stand in a queue
I'm not going told hold a door open for someone
The way that we all used to do

I'm not going to give up my seat anymore
When an Old person gets on the bus
I know it's sounds rough but now I've had enough
Of trying to turn them into us

What happened to just saying sorry
When you step onto somebody's foot
Or at least acknowledging somebody's presence
When did courtesy get overlooked

Now I'm not just talking about visitors
Or newcomers to our fair shores
But also the youngsters, who ought to know better
Neighbours of mine and of yours

Well, I'll probably still wave a quick, "Cheers Mate"
When someone lets me cross the road
And I'll likely say Thank You when I'm served my coffee
And smile and try not to explode

On second thoughts, No, I won't change what I do
Because taking my manners is theft
I may not be able to turn them into us
But at least I'll still walk on the left

Me and the Wife ...

Sit down while I tell you a story
It's about a day in the life
Of someone who we, are gonna call me
And someone else I call my wife

We'll start with the story of Mary
Who's already gone to the gym
She goes ev'ry morning around about dawning
That's how we both stay so slim

Now when I say both it's an aggregate
A bit like a joint Bank account
She works out and, drops a couple of pounds
And I put on two,.. It don't count

She says I should join her there one day
I'd love it, She tells me with glee
I don't know 'bout that, 'cos some of this fat
Well it's almost become part of me

By now you can see, that the story of me...
...and my wife's, one of light and of dark
She treats her body just like it's a temple
And mine's more a Disneyland park

So ends today's little story
A story of fitness and health
A story of life, of me and my wife
And you also may recognise yourself .....

Manflu ...

I've got what the ladies call Manflu
But that doesn't mean I'm not sick
I'm sneezing and coughing, I'm hot then I'm cold
And my head feels uncommonly thick

Now ladies, I know that it's funny
To watch us men suffer and stress
And lay on the sofa, wrapped in a duvet
Making the sounds of distress

We ask for a sandwich, a nice cup of tea
And a biscuit if you wouldn't mind
Have we got any Bourbons or Chocolate Digestives?
You know they are my favourite kind

But sympathy isn't forthcoming
You just do that eye rolling thing
Get it yourself, can't you see that I'm busy
Who died and made you the King?

But you know you'll be sorry, when nothing will fix it
No lotion, no potion, or pill
'Cause just like it says, on Spike Milligan's headstone
See, "I Said I Was Ill"

Maybe it's Because I'm a Londoner ...

Maybe It's Because I'm a Londoner,
Or Maybe London is because of Me
London is some buildings and a river
Like many other cities, you'll agree

If London has a magic, it's the people
All of us and those that came before
Charlie Dickens, Mary Shelley, My old Mum and your Aunt Nellie
Samuel Pepys and shoe-less Sandy Shaw

You can't ignore the beauty of the city
A jewel placed in this Green and Pleasant land
From Tower Bridge to Battersea from Wimbledon to Wem-be-ly
From Docklands in the east and up the Strand

I love the City's theatres and museums
Palaces and parks and so much more
People from all nations come to see them
And we have all this just outside our door

But think about the people that have made it what it is
Norman Foster, Alfred Hitchcock, Captain Bligh
David Beckham, Honor Blackman,HRH and Jasper Conran
You and me and even Stephen Fry

So born and bred or here by choice
all Londoners have their own voice
Now pick a card and play it as you see
Maybe It's Because I'm A Londoner
Or Maybe London is because of me...

Not Enough Time ...

There don't seem to be enough hours in the day
Come to that, enough day's in the week
It seems as though it was Monday yesterday
But it's Thursday again as we speak

I seem to have so many things to do
It's hard trying to fit it all in
What with the shopping and cooking and Golf
I just don't know where to begin

Go into the garden and water the flowers?
Or go 'round and visit my Mum?
Go to the range? well I know it sounds strange
But Lord knows how I'll get it all done

I'm up bright and early, to make the day longer
But that only gets me inspired
I never knew, there was so much to do
When you were Kind of Retired

Well anyway, I'd better get started
I tell you, It's tough being Me
I'll just make my plan, and do what I can
Of course, After a nice cup of tea ...xx

What Page I'm On ...

As I get older, Living,I find,
is a bit like reading a book
Where once in a while I flip back through pages,
just for a cursory look

It's not that I've lost it, or don't know what's happening
or even that anything's wrong
It's really much more like my bookmark's fell out
and I'm checking for what page I'm on

It may seem to some that I'm starting,
to slide down that slippery slope,
Of, I can't remember and What was his name?
and I'm heading for life's bottom rope

But of course that's not so, my memory's fine,
although it sometimes needs a nudge
I may not remember what I went upstairs for
but still recall Bootsie and Snudge

I think what I need is a Stocktake
and a clearout of some of the stuff
That I keep in my head, year upon year
It's time now enough is enough

Who cares about Binary numbers
or that Paul Daniel's real name is Ted
It's taking up valuable space that I need,
but somehow got stuck in my head

....

....

So, Ive got some facts to get rid of,
If anyone wants them at all
I've got the dates of the Wars of the Roses
and loads of stuff I learned at school

I know all the words to Mull of Kintyre
and where Winston Churchill grew up
My thirteen times table, Kane's brother was Able
and Old Shep, when he was a pup

I'll throw in some stuff about Star Wars
that I never wanted to know
The registration number of my brothers first car
and the way to Amarillo

Now after that memory clearout
and although I did keep lots of spares
I'm still none the wiser and still can't remember
just what I was doing upstairs...

Wednesday ...

If you've got tied up in your Duvet.
And somehow can't get out of bed
Why not turn off the Alarm clock radio
And stay there in comfort instead

There's nothing that special to get up for
It's only Wednesday after all
And you know what they say about Wednesday's
If you've seen one then you've seen them all

No, you're right, Get up and get at 'em
'Cos what if today is the day
You've waited for so long for something to happen
You don't want to miss it that way

Well okay then it might be tomorrow
And by then it'll be Friday eve
The weekend is coming and ev'rything's humming
See what happens if you just believe

So come on hold hands and play nicely
'Cos we're all going out on the town
Remember to wear your clean underwear
Like your Mum said, You might get knocked down

Trains ...

Where do they go to, those lines without end?
Just over that hill, just 'round that bend?
To faraway places with strange sounding names,
Or was that just a song, and my mind's playing games

No, I'm sure they go somewhere that I'd like to go,
Up in the mountains to play in the snow
Or down to the coast for a dip in the sea
I'm sure they go somewhere that I'd like to be

I'll buy me a ticket and jump on a train
I'll stop where it stops then get off again
Oh for the romance of riding the rails
The pull of the engine up hills and down dales

Is it nostalgia that takes me away
To black and white movies, back in the day
Steam trains and fedoras and a long ago time
Stolen kisses on platforms,
Brief encounters, sublime

It may be nostalgia
It may not be real
But the sound of the wheels
And the speed makes you feel
That those day's are not over
And like castles in Spain
They're just waiting for us
To discover again

Fifty Nine Summers ...

I am a man of Fifty Nine Summers
And Autumns and Winters and Springs
So as you can see I've been here for a while
And I've seen quite a few different things

I've been to some places and mixed with some faces
Rubbed shoulders with Rich and with Poor
With Gents and with Ladies, with good guys and baddies
Been positive and not been too sure

Of course, I've been younger and I have to say stronger
But I'd like to think never more wise
I've laughed and I've cried, but all that aside
I'm amazed still at just how time flies

Wasn't it yesterday that I turned Eighteen?
Or Twenty One, Thirty or Forty?
And how long ago was that Christmas Panto
When we laughed 'cos the clown had been naughty

I'm sure it's no more than a couple of years
Since my Son took his first breath of air
But now I'm a Grandad and trust me that's not bad
But how did that time disappear

As the man said, Regrets, I've had a few
After Fifty Nine Years I'm sure you would too
The good times have vastly outweighed the bad
But where has the time gone since I was a lad

I know I'm not done yet, I've a long way to go
And I'm first to admit that there's lots I don't know
But before we hear from the pipes and the drummers
Can you tell me what happened to those Fifty Nine Summers??

Cooking ...

I must admit I quite like cooking
But some terms I don't understand
So I thought I'd ask you, about One or two
Perhaps you could give me a hand

For example the first one is "Pan fried"
What else could you fry something in?
And then Oven Baked, now for Heavens sake
Where else would a Baking begin?

I realise that these are new ones
But there's old ones that I don't get too
How much is a pinch or some or a bit
Amounts that your Mum once told you

Now, I'm not a Meat and two veg man
I embrace the exotic with zeal
I once put an apple into a Chilli
Although I did take off the peel

I quite like the Hairy Bikers
And they tell me Nigella cooks too
I'll look out for that, next time she's on
Oh Yeah, Tell me, what is a Jus?

The other strange one is a Coulis
Oh yeah and a Salad Niçoise
I don't really care but I just thought I'd mention
That Sometimes they just do it for laughs

I'm off now to do tonight's dinner
I think we'll have something with chips
Now there is a saying I do understand
It ends ... a lifetime on the hips

Why can't I just win the Lottery ...

Why can't I just win the Lottery
About Half a Million would do
I'm not being greedy or asking for much
Just to do all the things i want to

I don't need to live like Rod Stewart
I'd just like enough to retire
And go to nice places with Samsonite cases
And all things to which we aspire

I'd like a two Bedroom apartment in Spain
And stay there for part of the year
Well maybe three bedrooms so the kids can come over
And not just when we are back here

But I'd still want to go to Hawaii
San Francisco and Florida too
So maybe I'll need a bit more that I thought
Maybe a Million or two

And then there's the cars, I do love a Bentley
And the Mrs said she'd like a Jag
My Son wants a Porche My Grandaughter a Merc
And My Brother wants an old Triumph Stag

....

Of course friends and family will need helping out
With Mortgage Repayments and stuff
Adding this up I'm beginning to wonder
If two Million Pounds is enough

Three maybe Four could be nearer the mark
But for comfort's sake Five will be nice
But let's make it ten So never again
Will I have to ask what is the price

Why can't I just win the Lottery
But only the Euros will do
With seventeen million in my back pocket
I promise I'll share some with you ....

She was a Dancer ...

She was a dancer, the world at her feet
He played guitar at the place they would meet
After the show when nobody was there
She'd dance for him and he'd play for her

She loved his music and she loved him too
He was transfixed by the way she would move
Graceful and rhythmic an angel on earth
He played his six strings for all he was worth

With feet and with fingertips aching and sore
They'd sit and drink coffee and talk until four
Then says their good nights and go out in the rain
And live for the day they would do this again

They talked about life, the future, their dreams
Everything there for the taking it seemed
Together forever it couldn't go wrong
While she had her dancing and he played her song

Time marches on as in everyone's life
He became Husband and she became Wife
Things get forgotten as life moves so fast
Late nights romancing a thing of the past

Three children later a life been and gone
Now just the two of them, Darby and Joan
But some things don't change and as ever today
When everyone's gone, She'll dance and he'll play

Sam ...

Today is the twenty first of March
There's a story that needs to be told
It's all about my best mate Sam
And today he is Forty years old

Now don't ask me how that happened
I'm sorry, I haven't a clue
A full grown man with kids of his own
From that little lad that I knew

We grew up together like brothers
Though he's twenty years younger than me
I remember so well, his first day at school
And the first time he sat on my knee

When he fractured his leg playing football
And the day that he bought his first car
To the look on his face when his first child was born
And the first time we went to a bar

I'm sure I've forgotten to mention,
That my best mate is also my Son
A Man any Dad would be proud of
And a Dad who's second to none

And very soon he'll be a Grandad
And the circle just goes 'round again
Don't worry Son, we'll get through it together
I Love you now as I did then

The Storyteller ...

There's an old man who lives by the river
With stories to make your teeth itch
Stories of bad times, of good times and sad times
Of poor rubbing shoulders with rich

Nobody knows just how old he is
In his braces and collarless shirt
I'm sure if you asked him how much time has passed him
He'd tell you he's older than dirt

He'll tell you a tale for a glass of brown ale
Or a coffee if the morning is cold
A warriors story, of days filled with glory
And of days long before he was old

His stories go back to a bygone era
To fighting the fascists in Spain
Then coming back home to the bombing of London
And then heading for Europe again

The bridge at Remagen, The Beaches of Dunkirk
Some stories borrowed, Some blue
That summer in Rome and the girls back at home
Some of them may even be true

Then through the fifties in his blue velvet drape
When he sung for his supper and more
He may even mention without real intention
That he dated a Young Sandie Shaw

....

....

He says that he worked as a roadie
In the sixties for the Beatles and the Stones
And that he wrote, a massive hit song
Recorded by Mr Tom Jones

Why Why Why would he lie
When Google will tell us the truth
Maybe he did but we don't know his name,
So how could we find any proof

If you add it all up chronologically
Then he's two days older than God
But buy him a coffee and sit for a while
'Cos he's not just some silly old sod

The point is sometimes he exaggerates
Just like the rest of us do
But remember one day, with a following wind
The old man may just well be you

The Old Cemetery ...

We used to play in here among the tombstones
Climbing trees and hiding from our mates
Fifty years have come and passed but memories that fade so fast
Came flooding back as I stepped through the gates

Little boys on bikes became the Cowboys in the movies
Or International Rescue for the day
Pantomimes for Simpler times, Imaginations undefined
And all played out one side of Hamlets Way

Reading out the names on all the Gravestones
Telling scary stories to our friends
Then someone climbs the Conker Tree, there's one for you and one for me
And the Conker World Cup Final starts again

The Cemo, as we called it, was our own adventure playground
Our Summer days were spent in it's delights
But broken stones, imagined moans, fallen trees and Garden Gnomes
Were scary on those cold dark Winter nights

I'm glad to see that once again the place is being used
And so much that I remember stays the same
Maybe, with a change of clothes, this little boy from Southern Grove
Can Holler "Hi Ho Silver" once again ...

The Dyson ...

I've broken the hose on my Dyson
The one that goes "Right up the stairs"
The one that pulls faces at hard to reach places
Well I must have caught mine unawares

The coily bit came out of the whassname
And I can't get the flippin' thing in
The prongs have snapped off and the press thing is lost
Let the search for a spare part begin

Now shopping on line ain't my first choice
I'm more of an old fashioned guy
I like to walk out with it under my arm
Like the old days Try before you buy

But I fire up the laptop and go searching
More in hope than experience would suggest
There seems such a lot, what model have I got?
I'm not sure and so I just guessed

I've got the Ball type, the one for all floors
Oh I see, that's the old one, now which one fits yours?
Is it the Coupé with the extra wide wheels?
Or the four on the floor gears .. Well that's how it feels

Well, I've ordered it now and paid for it
And all I can do now is wait
I should have got Mary to do it really
Oh bugger, D'you think it's too late ? .....

The Dishwasher ...

I'm getting the hang of the dishwasher
And using it like everyone else
So after my Tea, no more wash up for me
'cos the cups go in on the top shelf

I'm getting the hang of it, plates on the bottom
And in goes the measuring cup
Cutlery into the basket below
I'm amazed at how quick it fills up

But everything has to be rinsed over first
And the saucepans? .. It won't get that off
So I'll just do the ones that I think are the worst
With some Fairy and a washing up cloth

Well, while I've got a sink full of suds
I'll just wash the glasses by hand
And my favourite cup, I'll just wash and hang up
Just for convenience you understand

And then when it's done and you open it
It takes ages to put everything away
I'm getting the hang of the dishwasher
But not using it Every day

The Swing ...

My Golfing buddy called and said he can't come out to play
But my clubs are already in my bag so I'll go anyway
I think I'll go and Ride the Range while practicing my swing
'Til I can swing like Frank Sinatra used to swing and sing

But that's a different kind of swing and my Golf swing isn't strong
It's almost like my swing is swung, It never lasted long
The first time that I played nine holes, I got two holes in par
But now my Drive has took a dive unless I'm in my car

I need to keep my head still and of course my left arm straight
Almost stand on the balls of my feet to balance out the weight
Stick my bum out, arch my back, 'til I look like a pregnant duck
Steady back then follow through and hit it... with any luck

So anyway that's me today, Swinging and shaking my head
Smiling when I get it right, or swearing under my breath
The only thing I can say to this game is "I've got you under my skin"
Now we're back on Frank Sinatra and Boy that man could swing

Spring Cleaning ...

The Children all love the Tooth Fairy
He leaves money under their pillows
Father Christmas leaves them presents
Everywhere he goes

The Easter Bunny's just as welcome
Leaving things chocolate and sweet
They let themselves in and then leave again
But leave the place tidy and neat

But there is another little bugger
Who often comes into my house
Not quite as nice as the others
But really as quiet as a mouse

Well I'm gonna call him "The Dust Bunny"
But he's certainly no friend of mine
He spreads all his dust, So housework's a must
But at bed time last night it looked fine

So tell me, where does this dust come from?
Does he buy it somewhere by the bag?
And why does he spread it 'round my house
It's proper becoming a drag

Now I don't mind doing some housework
And I'm often found pushing the vacuum
But not every day, 'though I do have to say
I was sure that I'd just cleaned the bedroom

And how did my windows get dirty
Those net curtains could do with a preening
Oh well, It's March so I might as well start
To get on and do some Spring Cleaning

Slipstreaming ...

What is it with old folk and slipstreaming
You know when they walk on your heels
You're strolling along, minding your own
Then they're on you, well that's how it feels

They dawdle along, not a care in the world
'Til they see you and then pick up speed
They fall in with your pace, like an extra shoe lace
Or a shadow you don't really need

It's almost as if your pulling them along
Like they're caught in an invisible net
And don't even talk to me about when it's raining
You're soaked and they're not even wet

I'm sure that they're just being nosy
And listening to my conversation
I talk to the wife about our personal life
And you can hear there exasperation

But next time it happens I'll get them
I'll turn and walk back up the street
Mind you then they'll be facing me
And likely to tread on my feet ....

Bless 'em .....

Turning Sixty ...

A mate of mine turned sixty at the weekend
And although I beat him by a month or two
When you see it happen, to those you went to school with
It kinda hammers home the point to you

Sixty, flippin' sixty, well, that's how the numbers run
You're doing fine when you're fifty nine and then comes another one
Now don't get me wrong, in the words of the song,
I'm livin' la vida loca
But at sixty years old, you don't need to be told,
That there'll be no more playing Strip Poker

You don't chase after a bus anymore,
And you don't chase after the girls
Either they come to you or you've missed that one too
And that's just the way it unfurls

Now I'm not saying sixty is ancient,
Or even that it's over the hill
You know what they say in their "off the cuff" way,
You're only as old as you feel

So, to all who were born, in the year of our Lord,
Nineteen hundred and fifty and five
You are, or you're gonna be sixty this year
And I'll tell you know how to survive

....

....

Don't mix with anyone younger than you
And holiday in old peoples places
They call you young man, when they can't and you can
And don't carry big, heavy cases

Don't make a plan with a much younger man,
To go running, in the morning at seven
Running's a mistake, you don't want to make
But if you do make it more like eleven

So as you turn sixty, just like me and Richie,
Then do it with style and good grace
Don't fear the cold because sixty's not old
But carry a coat ....just in case

The Thingy ...

I can't seem to get the thingy to turn
The whassnames come out of the thing
It's making a sound but it just won't go 'round
It's whistling and trying to sing

The doo dah is twisted and won't sit in straight
I don't know how it goes back in
It's very annoying 'cos I was just toying
With the idea of buying it's twin

I thought I'd have one for a back up
In case something ever went wrong
But now I don't know, but I do need it though
I should have had two all along

Well I'll have to get on without it
And just go to work as I am
But I'll worry all day, Do you know a way?
To help me get out of this jam

Oh never mind, It don't matter
And worse things happen at sea
I'll come home tonight, and by then it just might,
Be working, we'll just have to see

The Thingy (Part Two) ...

I've found out what's wrong with the thingy
It wasn't the whassname at all
It seems that the spindle had started to dwindle
And my spare cotter pin was too small

I needed some new tools to fix it
So I went to the shop and I bought
A left handed screwdriver, that cost me a fiver
And an extendable shaft of some sort

It seems or at least so they tell me
That you need and adjustable spanner
And a blue Thingybob, that might do the job
Or sixteen pound long handled hammer

Well I took out the what do you call it
And you won't believe what happened next
I broke off the knob with the blue thingybob
And that left me a little bit vexed

So I took out the hammer and whacked it
But honestly that wasn't the answer
What do you know...It dropped on my toe
That could end my career as a dancer

I know that I should buy a new one
But I'm a waste not want not kind of guy
It may not be mended just as nature intended
But you can't say that I didn't try ....

Top of the Stairs ...

There was an old man who lived life without care
Who stood for a moment, on the top stairs
Was he going upstairs or coming back down?
He couldn't remember so he just turned around

I might as well go to the loo while I'm here
He said to himself as he but he wasn't quite clear..
..why the cistern was filling in the bathroom unseen
It was then that he realised, that's where he's just been

Well, that drama over he headed back down
He was on the sixth step when he just turned around
And realised that he'd left his glasses up there
So that's when he started,... back up the stairs

He soon found his glasses, they were there by the pipe
But he couldn't see through them, they needed a wipe
So he went to the bedroom for his polishing cloth
Breathed on them and wiped them and got the marks off

With his glasses now sparkling he put them back on
It was then that he noticed his wristwatch was gone
Now where was I last time I saw it ? he wondered
Then remembered that he'd come upstairs unencumbered

I'll go down to the Kitchen, it must be down there
And again he was standing, at the top of the stairs
Was he going upstairs or coming back down
He couldn't remember so he just turned around...

Roman Road ...

There's a road in the East End, that we all well know
It runs between Bethnal Green station and Bow
I've lived in it, shopped in it, drunk in it's pubs
I once crashed my scooter there, outside Harbuds

From Cambridge Heath Road, past the new fire station
To the place where the Buddhists all go for salvation
A slight dog leg left, by where Davis's was
To the Weavers and Zack's and Market Square buzz

There's Daycocks and Whistles and the Cranbrook Estate
Past the old Beehive and keep going straight
Over the hill and then down to the lights
The Aberdeen used to be there, on the right

There's Thompson's down there, where they sell everything
The White Horse was opposite, where my Dad used to sing
Down to The Albert where the street market starts
And the Pie and Mash shop, always close to my heart

Now, where was the record shop? that's right, over there
There was Cohen's and Byrites for something to wear
Caters and Woolworth's and the stalls overflowed
We all have our memories of our Roman Road

The Wireless ...

Do you remember listening to the Wireless
Before the Television was the King
Two way Family Favourites, Music While You Work
And waiting for Petula Clark to sing

The Navy Lark, The Goons and Tony Hancock
Mrs Dale, The Archers and Housewives Choice
Billy Cotton's Bandshow, Little Jimmy Clitheroe
Knowing who was who by just their voice

We laughed and cried and marvelled at the stories
As we listened sitting in our Nan's Front Room
The wireless was our Window on life's Glories
From Kennedy to Landing on the Moon

The Wireless taught me songs that I remember
The songs that helped to make me who I am
Morningtown Ride and This Is My song
And Tulips From Amsterdam

Sparky's Magic Piano, Nellie and Little White Bull
Puff The Magic Dragon, as kids we loved them all
The world it opened up to us seemed endless
Do you remember listening to the wireless ??

Who We Are ...

When the docks were still open in the East End of London
And your Mum used to walk you to school
The shops were all closed for the whole day on Sunday
And only your Ice Cream was cool

Football and Runouts and Hop Scotch and Kiss Chase
Were the games that we played in the street
Trainers were people who trained you for something
Not something you wore on your feet

When your Mum used to shout out your name from the door
And you knew it was time to go home
When you dialled someones number and pressed button A
On a great big black Bakelite Phone

When you bought a Red Rover and got on a Bus
And didn't come home until dark
And on long Summer Sundays, your Mum and your Dad
Would take you out over the park

When your bath and your Toilet were out in the back yard
And Max Bygraves was still a big star
Those were the days, as everyone says
That made us all now who we are

Linda Rinder...

Linda Rinder, Looked through the Window
Wondering where it went wrong
She expected so much when she married a judge
And they hadn't been married that long

Everything went so well at the start
But she had a strange sense of humour
They said that she once kicked a copper up the arse
But he thought it was only a rumour

He hated the first day of April
While she loved a practical joke
Once while he was cooking and he wasn't looking
She'd filled the whole room full of smoke

She lead him a dance when she got the chance
And it started to get on his nerves
When she egged his car, she'd gone just too far
Now she'd get just what she deserved

She didn't think he would send her to prison
When he dressed in his wig and his silk
It was only in fun, when she done what she done
She'd put Pepper in the Cat's milk

Well they say that forgiveness is good for the soul
And after a month she got out on parole
They're trying again and so far it's easy
Just her and the Judge and their little cat .... Sneezy

Magic Bus ...

Climb aboard the magic bus
And journey with the rest of us
We're heading off down Thursday Street
Come to the back, I've saved you a seat

There's no need to pack 'cos we're coming right back
And we'll have you all home before dark
The radio's playing your favourite song
As we take you once more 'round the park

The bus is painted, Red, White and Blue
The wheels are round and the windows are too
With flags and bunting all put there for you
As we head out into the unknown

Tomorrow is Friday and then the weekend
Lets get in the mood for it now
It's summer, why not show the world what you've got
Use Thursday as your finest hour

So with a spring in your step, a song in your heart
A smile on your lips as we wait to depart
And if someone upsets you don't take it to heart
We're all on the Magic Bus

Old Man, Tell us a Story ...

Old Man tell us a story,
Tell us of when you were young
What was it like when you were a lad,
Sing us the songs that you sung

When a young Frank Sinatra was making his way
The Glen Miller sound that made ev'ryone sway
Happy Birthday Mr President from Marylin's lips
And that boy Elvis Presley was shaking his hips

Tell us again how you fought in a war
And what it was like when it ended
How you came home and just started again
Or is it least said soonest mended

Tell us your stories of loves won and lost
Of fashions and what car did you drive
What did a gallon of petrol cost then
And of struggling just to survive

Tell us your tales set in simpler times
Of "Walking My Baby Back Home"
Of letters and bus fare and meeting up somewhere
'Cos no-one you knew had a phone

Going to dances and making advances
Stories you've told us before
Living in two rooms upstairs in your Mum's house
And having your Nan live next door

....

....

Because your life story's our story
We are now who you were back then
And when the next generation grows up
We'll tell all your stories again

These stories are not told for your sake
But for us and for lest we forget
That nobody said life was gonna be easy
But what you put in's what you get

Old folk are our social history
And so often they're heroes unsung
Old Man tell us a story
Tell us of when you were young

Bethnal Green ...

I wasn't born in Bethnal Green but it's been my stomping ground
I lived there once or twice and somehow always stuck around
In 1970 - 71 when we were the go getters
Up and down the Roman Road on Vespas and Lambrettas

Lou's cafe for a cup of tea, there was no Starbucks then
Ride to the bottom of Bethnal Green Road, turn and ride back again
Then time moved on, the scooters gone the White Hart was our haunt
The Wimpy Bar, a fitting place for any débutante

The Green Gate on a Tuesday night, the comics made us laugh
York Hall on a Saturday our weekly Turkish bath
Blackman's down in Cheshire St. for our new Desert boots
Sunday night we'd be alright in our Double breasted suits

The years went by and so did I and Tipples came our way
When Linen suits and Espadrilles were the order of the day
Saturday night was ladies night we'd go somewhere else instead
Wherever we'd go you'd always know we'd end in the Camdens Head

I've lived there played, there, worked there stayed there
and of all the places that I've been
I've come to the conclusion that all in all. ...
I quite like Bethnal Green ...

You Didn't Know Me Then ...

I haven't always been this old
I haven't always felt this cold
Time was I was young and bold
You didn't know me then

I didn't always look this way
I didn't always sleep all day
I used to dance the night away
You didn't know me then

You never knew the Troubadour
Who fell in love with the girl next door
Who sung for her chanson d'amour
You didn't know me then

You never knew the Warrior
The Lover or the friend
You never knew My Glory days
You didn't know me then

Don't judge me now by what you see
Don't Judge on what you think is me
I was you before you were me
You didn't know me then

It's true my youth has left me
But I'm sure you will allow
That if you didn't know me then
Then you don't know me now

Closer to Heaven ? ...

I was out for a walk on a warm summers day
When I stopped at a bench for a rest
My Dad came along and sung me a song
About something, somewhere in the west

Then a woman I knew said, may I listen too
As she sat there cross legged on the ground
I really must say what a beautiful day
Except for that strange humming sound

My wife cycled by with her sister
I think they were going to Church
Then a man in a hat said do you fancy a chat
And strangely I felt the world lurch

My Nan told a story about driving a lorry
Along the coast down by Pevensey bay
And a dog on a skateboard looked over and said
That's something you don't see everyday

After all that I was thirsty
And felt as though somebody nudged me
Then vaguely I heard someone whisper the words
Do you fancy a nice cup of tea

The low humming sound then got louder
As I came to my senses again
I soon realised as I opened my eye's
That I'd fallen asleep on the plane

I laughed to myself at the dream I'd just had
A disjointed adventure and seeing my Dad
When you dream on a plane it's strange who you meet
Closer to heaven at thirty thousand feet? ...

Constant Companion ...

I had a near constant companion
For something like forty odd years
A skinny white chap with a little brown cap
Who saw me through laughter and tears

He was always there to chill me out
When the stresses of life got me down
He was always on hand, while singing on stage
Or just playing guitar in the lounge

We travelled the world together
From the States to the Isle of Capri
It didn't cost too much to take him
'Cos he always went duty free

But some people said he was anti social
And just didn't want him around
Fed up with seeing, him and his mates
Crushed out and laid on the ground

Our relationship ended some three years ago
Before the wife started to nag
But I have to admit on mornings like this
I sometimes just fancy a fag.....

Cats and Dogs ...

A cat is a cat and that's pretty much that
But a dog, well now that's something else
There's big ones and small ones, short ones and tall ones
But they don't tend to fend for themselves

A dog won't go looking for sparrows
He'll just sit there and wait 'til he's fed
A cat will just look at whatever you've cooked
And go bring you a dead frog instead

Now, while cats come in various colours
And I know there's a couple of posh breeds
A cat is a cat is a cat is a cat
And take care of themselves and their needs

A cat owner will tell you that their cat is clever
And a dog is as dumb as barbed wire
But a dog is more loyal and won't act like a royal
While he sits at your feet by the fire

But a dog needs a bath and a haircut
And grooming and all stuff like that
Just try putting your feline in a bath full of saline
You could end up wearing your cat

You don't take a cat out for walkies
And a dog don't go prowling at night
But a dog will stand by you and a cat will come home
As long as you treat them both right

Changing Tastes ...

I find as I get older, that I quite like marzipan
A taste I couldn't suffer when I was a younger man
It made me start to wonder how a preference just appears
As we go along our way and onward through the years

I always hated vegetables, greens of any kind
But when deciding what to have for dinner, now I find..
..I'm looking for the Broccoli and even Cauliflower
I used to go for all that's sweet but now I favour sour

I always chose milk chocolate, but now I go for plain
And as for sugar in my tea, I won't do that again
I actually quite like the fact that nothing stays forever
But there's one thing I have to say, that seems to leave me never

I still don't like Alarm Clocks,... they all go off to soon
I lay there in my reverie and then the next thing BOOM
My sleep is taken from me by a nasty ringing sound
My eyes are still shut tight but I am slowly coming 'round

But then again the bright side is, they bring a brand new day
It brought us this one, but I'm sure, there is a gentler way
Enjoy yourself and go about your business as you do
And if you Alarm Clock hasn't gone off yet,
Who's reading this to you ? .....

Cowboy ...

I'm fed up with driving in London
And with this winter weather of course
My wipers have rotted, in the rain we've been having
That wouldn't happen if I rode a horse

I've always fancied, being a Cowboy
I guess I was just born too late
Maybe I would be the sheriff
And I'd deputise all of my mates

I'd wear a white hat like Big Gary Cooper
And ride into town like John Wayne
Get down off of my horse and drink my milk
Get back on and ride out again

I'd eat my baked beans round a campfire
And fart like a trooper all night
And play my guitar, under the stars
And give those coyotes a fright

But I guess now that's not going to happen
Well, let's face it I'm sixty years old
And riding the range on a horse ain't too comfy
And I'm sure the nights can get quite cold

So it's into the car and and turn on the wipers
And drive out through London again
Maybe I should leave, the flipping thing here
And just let the train take the strain

I've always fancied being a Train Driver........

But that's another story..

Dan, The Handy Man ...

She was scrolling through the classifieds and found a Handy Man
She dialled the number and a voice said "Hi my name is Dan"
She'd somehow found her ex husband, He never saw that coming
But maybe she should ask him to come round and fix her plumbing

No that's not a euphemism it's just that her toilet's broke
She tried before to get it fixed but just got some strange bloke
Who'd seen too many movies about plumbers and bored housewives
Honestly is this the way some people live their lives?

So anyway, When Dan came round, the spark was all but gone
But with this close proximity some things don't take too long
Familiarity breeds contempt but absence makes the heart grow fonder
And it wasn't long before he took her out for a ride on the back of his Honda

They rode around the country lanes, it was lovely day
They parked up by the burger van and got a take away
She had a hot dog, he had a burger, they both had a can of coke
And somewhere under the shade of a tree, they shared a private joke

A bit later on they went back to her flat, and one thing led to another
It didn't take long before the con - versation got round to her Mother
How's your Mum? He asked her, is her broomstick primed and ready
It's nearly time for Halloween and we wouldn't want her being unsteady

That's not funny Dan and she's coming round soon so you'd better be on your way
Can you imagine if she found you here? Imagine just what she would say
So Dan up and left and they smiled at each other he walked out of there unescorted
She smiled a contented smile to herself, at least she'd got her plumbing sorted

And as he left, their thoughts exchanged though not a word was spoken
Laughing about that last euphemism
'Cos her flippin' toilet's still broken ......

The Pirate ...

I could have been a pirate,
and sailed the seven seas
With a red bandanna, wrapped 'round my head,
and trousers rolled up to my knees

I'd learn to play the squeeze-box
and I'd play those pirate tunes
I'd have my treasure buried
in a box of gold doubloons

I could have been a Pirate
with a huge tri cornered hat
And a parrot on my shoulder,
Now what d'you think of that ?
I'd sail off in The Flying Dutchman,
heading towards the sun
With my motley crew and a yo ho ho
and of course a bottle of rum

I'd sail the Caribbean
stopping off just now and then
Pick up some more treasure
and the head off once again
The Jolly Roger flying
from the top of our huge mast
Firing Cannonballs at other ships
as they went past

I could have been a pirate,
in the Long John Silver style
I'd call out Aharrr Jim lad
and you hear it for a mile
I'd outrun all the other ships,
using every sailors trick
But the only trouble with all this ? ...
I tend to get Seasick

New Shoes ...

It's raining here in London
And I'm wearing my new shoes
I thought well why not, you've got what you've got
And today I've got nothing to lose

I bring up the shoes in a Cavalier manner,
Have I even mentioned them yet?
I've got time to tell ya 'Cos I've popped into Costa
To keep them from getting too wet

I went shopping in Lakeside yesterday
And went into Jones of all places
And in front of my eyes, and in my size,
A pair of Tan brogues with Mauve laces

It was love at first sight so I thought that I might,
try them on just to see how they'd fit
They felt very nice and then I saw the price
And had to find somewhere to sit

Well after some thought and deep breathing
And knowing the mortgage was paid
I haven't spent all my redundancy yet
And Mary did not look afraid

I parted with the necessary
And put them both on straight away
In order to get my money's worth,
I'll wear these bad boys every day

So I'll say to my Son and Grandchildren,
I wish I could see all your faces
When my last will is read and there's no money, instead. ...
You get a pair of Tan Brogues with Mauve laces

Nostalgia's a Thing of the Past ...

I love watching black and white movies
and seeing pictures from back in the day
I love reminiscing on things that we're missing
And remembering games that we'd play

Listening to the music of the fifties and sixties,
And recalling the feel of the times
Tasting again things that ain't quite the same
Like Caramac and Chocolate Limes

I used to love Nut Crunch and Cracknell,
Bar Six and Sweet Cigarettes
Aztec and Tiffin and Parisian Creams ...
All things you can no longer get

Gerry and the Pacemakers, Billy J Kramer,
Johnnie Ray and Cilla Black too
Young Patsy Cline was a favourite of mine
And Joe Brown had a Picture of You

Hop Scotch and Run-outs, hiding in Dugouts,
A day at the seaside with Mum
Radio Caroline, Sunburn and Calamine
And packs of Beech Nut Chewing Gum

Two Tone Suits and Desert Boots
And memories of people now passed
Great days indeed but then so are these,
Nostalgia's a thing of the past

...and She Wonders ...

...and she wonders if he ever thinks about her
And he wonders why he ever let her go
She remembers all the times he said he loved her
And he wishes, somehow he could let her know

He keeps her photo in his inside pocket
While, she stares at her phone for hours on end
She grabs and smells his shirt, still in her closet
He dials but puts the handset down again

If only he could find a way to tell her
If only she could hold him just once more
She misses him so very much, he was her first and only love
He'd love to stand again at her front door

It's been a year or so since he last saw her
She wondered if he'd changed much over time
She practised every day, if she saw him, what she'd say
His only thought, I wish she was still mine

She thought by now he'd probably found another
He wondered if she wore a wedding ring
She sat there watching T.V. on that Sunday afternoon
And suddenly her phone began to ring ...

The Café ... Part One ...

He sits in the Café, drinking his Coffee
He's sat there for such a long time
She works in the Café, serving his Coffee
She whispers "I wish he was mine"

Every morning, a large Cappuccino
And sometimes a Croissant and jam
Every morning she wonders and whispers
"Does he even know who I am"

He'd say "Good Morning, How are you today?"
"May I have a large Cappuccino"
He didn't notice, she knew what he wanted
And had the cup ready to go

Sometimes he'd tease her while trying to please her
"I like it like me, Big and Strong ?"
But as she approaches, she'd suddenly notices
He held her gaze just a little too long

Then as he sits down, she hears a loud sound
It's a gong going off in her head
And she whispers softly, "Well, if he likes me...
...Then why on earth hasn't he said?"

She makes her plan, he will be her Man
While he's thinking in much the same way
We'll just wait and see, will it be He or She
Who makes their move the next day ....

The Café ...Part Two ...

He went to the Café, for his morning coffee
For today was to be the big day
She waited for him knowing when he came in
She'd say how she felt straight away

He said "Good Morning, How are you today?"
"May I have a large Cappuccino"
"And a croissant with Jam".. and then he saw the pram
As she followed is gaze she yelled.. "No"

"No?.. I can't have my coffee?".. he joked
And she panicked and stared at the ground
She stuttered and spluttered as his croissant was buttered
And he took it and went and sat down

"He thinks it's my baby" she whispered
She's got a baby, he thought
"I need to tell him, I'm just babysitting"
He stared at the coffee he'd brought

Then it occurred to him, I bet it's not hers
She's looking after it for somebody else
She whispered "I wish he'd look over this way"
"And then I could tell him myself"

He did make a try at catching her eye
But she was serving the building site crowd
She had something else that she needed to tell him
But Fridays were always so loud

"I wish he'd come over" she whispered
I can't leave the counter right now
Perhaps I should leave it 'til Monday, he thought
That seemed like a good plan somehow

The Café ...Part Three ...

He went to the Café, for more than just coffee
On this rain sodden Monday and he froze
He was soaked to the skin as he tried to get in
But the sign on the door just said Closed

Why didn't she tell me?, he thought to himself
She whispered "I hope that he's there"
He turned up his collar and wanted to holler
She brushed and then re-brushed her hair

Without too much fuss, she stepped off the bus
But got soaked by the bus and the spray
He stared at the door for a few seconds more
And he turned and then he walked away

She soon recognised him, hunched up against the rain
And although they weren't properly acquainted
She called out "I'm sorry, we're closed for the week,
The Café is being repainted"

He turned on his heels as he heard her
Her face seemed to glow in the rain
He walked back toward her, knowing he loved her
And she knew that she felt the same

....

....

He smiled when she told him that her name was Kate
He told her that his name was Billy
William and Kate ? ... It has to be fate
Surely thoughts of a wedding were silly

They chatted forever then set off together
Sharing her little umbrella
She told him all that she wanted to say
And he, all he wanted to tell her

Now they go to the Café for coffee together
And their first Baby's soon on her way
Their wedding wasn't in Westminster Abbey
But the Café was closed on that day ...

The Snows of Winter

I love the snows of winter
And it's laying on the ground
The strange light that reflects from it when evening comes around
The icicles that hang from ev'ry gutter in the street
The brightly coloured hats and scarves of people that we meet
The white capped boughs of naked trees, the still and frozen lakes
The beauty of the barren landscape only Winter makes

Then comes spring and April showers, the snow's been washed away
The chill has gone, the warm clothes too and Summer's on it's way
But let's not rush to bypass Spring and all it has in store
The promise of regeneration, new life and much more
The spread of golden daffodils, the new lambs find their feet
The fresh smells fill our senses and remind us life is sweet

The calender rolls round to June, and now the Summer's here
The sun is out, the sky is blue and we're all of good cheer
This is what we've waited for, the languid Summer days
The sultry nights with star-filled skies, the barbecues ablaze
The smell of fresh mown grass, the sounds of children having fun
Listening to The Beach Boys while you're sitting in the sun
Your hair is getting lighter and your skin a golden brown
Goodbye July and August and September comes around

And now we enter Autumn, Mother Nature can show off
She sets the trees afire with colour before the leaves fall off
She goes from red to yellow, stopping all along the way
With ev'ry shade of brown and gold and orange on display
But it's short lived for comes the wind, November comes to town
I love the snows of Winter, And Its Laying On The Ground.

A Borrowed Umbrella ...

Out for a stroll with a borrowed umbrella
In a soaking wet, rain sodden park
It's quarter past one, there's no sign of the sun
And the sky very quickly gets dark

The puddles reflecting the trees and the netting...
..that hangs limp from the basketball hoops
A man rushes by with his collar up high
As into the shelter he stoops

The children are splashing, their parents are dashing
To get them in out of the rain
And as they get under, the shelter the Thunder
Brings them out laughing again

And then there's a crack in the grey leaden sky
The sun's breaking through, It's beginning to dry
The rain goes away just as quick as it came
The umbrellas come down and are rolled up again

Ten minutes on and the clouds are all gone
The sky is a clear azure blue
The ground dries up fast as the rain now has passed
As our Summer does what our Summer's do

Bank Holiday Monday ...

Red Lorry, Yellow Lorry, Silver car then blue
Nose to tail and tailing back from here to Timbuktu
Heading somewhere going nowhere in a traffic jam
I wonder where they'd be if they weren't stuck here where I am

Nothing has moved now for at least half an hour
And most of the engines are turned off
It's eerily silent except for some kids
And a man with a terrible cough

The girl in the Mini scrunches her hair
And checks it in her rear view mirror
They guy with the wife and three screaming kids
Pretends that he just doesn't see her

There's a Volkswagen camper van on the hard shoulder
With two Hippy Chicks and a bloke
Sharing a cigarette, they can't have much money
But there's billows of strange smelling smoke

Then a young lad runs into the bushes
With his Mum walking closely behind
If you go down to the woods today
You never know what you might find

I aimlessly look at the car next to mine
As the driver then catches my eye
Thumbs off the steering wheel we both utter "Tut"
And roll ours eyes up to the sky

...

....

But hold on, what's that ? something's moving
I saw somebody waving their arm
No, a girl in bright clothes has seen someone she knows
And set off a whole false alarm

Still, Bank Holiday Monday is Bank Holiday Monday
And there's really no point in complaining
'cos all through this verse, It could be much worse
Yeah you know it, at least it's not raining ....

Slogans ...

We're programmed without really knowing
The things going into our heads
I know that that's true Or at least think I do
Or is it just what someone said

Can you tell Stork from Butter
Do you know that Beanz Meanz Heinz
For Mash Get Smash, Snap Crackle and Pop
And millions of other Tag Lines

It Refreshes the parts that others can't reach
And Bisto comes with an Ahh..
Have a Break Have a Kit Kat, you can Say It with Flowers
and Vorsprung Durch Technik your car

It's Finger Licking Good and Because I'm Worth It
and we all know that Coke's the Real Thing
You Love it or Hate it but as Nike say Just do It
It does Exactly what it says on the tin

These phrases have entered our language
To a greater or lesser degree
Go to work on an egg, Put a Tiger in your tank
And Shredded Wheat ?.. No-one has three

But I won't be fooled by their rhetoric
Or taken in by them one bit
Because I'm going out for a burger and chips
Do Do Do Do Doooo ... I'm Lovin' It

The Bath ...

When I was a nipper, and sat in the bath
I'd wash from my feet to my head
But when I got married, and the wife sat and laughed
And then shook her head and she said..

It's obvious you should always start at the top
And carefully work your way down
Start with you hair, that's up in the air
And finish up down on the ground

Now when she explained it, I did see her point
And I'd pretty much been unaware
That you don't want to wash your face with a flannel
That you've just been using elsewhere

So I changed the habits of a lifetime
But somehow it never seemed right
And after that day I mainly took showers
At least that is until last night

I got in the bath and just for a laugh
I first washed my tootsies and then
I washed up to my smile, which I kept for a while
'Cos I felt like a nipper again ...xx

Darth Vader's helmet ...

My Car looks like Darth Vader's helmet
At least that's what my neighbour said
I can't stop laughing, just thinking about it...
...Parked on old Darth Vader's Head

It's an old PT Cruiser, a bit of a bruiser
And it's all black and shiny of course
And after he said it, whenever I drive it
I feel like I'm feeling the force

So now when I go to the Dark Side (South London)
And trust me it's always a fluke
I'll give them a fright when I stop at a light...
...And say, "I am your Father Luke"

My Car looks like Darth Vader's helmet
And it's strange now that's all I can see
We'll be picking the Grandchildren up in it tonight
Obi-wan Kenobe and me ...

The youngest one calls it a Taxi
And the next one, Grandad's Batmobile
But from now we'll call it, Darth Vader's Helmet
And I'll be Han Solo at the wheel ....

If I Had a Bike ...

If I had a bike I'd go out cycling every morning
And I'd use it as a way of getting fit
I'd lose a load of weight and I'd soon get into shape
And before long I'd have muscles in my spit

If I had a bike I'd soon be built like David Beckham
And maybe get some tattoos on my back
Buns of steel, Abs like iron, fit as a fiddle, strong as a lion
And don't be surprised if you see the old six pack

If I had a bike, I'd take it with me to the seaside
And ride it up and down the promenade
I'd strap it to the roof-rack I'd have fitted to the car
'Cos cycling to the seaside would be hard

If I had a bike I'd go out wearing jeans and tee shirt
I couldn't see myself out wearing Lycra
To be honest with my shape and size It wouldn't be a real surprise
I'd look more like a dressed up Nissan Micra

If I had a bike I'd go out cycling in all weathers
And I don't want to sound unsportsmanlike
But the more I think about it I can really do without it
Thank the Lord I haven't got a bike

Not Now ... Back Then ...

What about a bit of fun?
A trip down memory lane
I know we've been down there before
But let's go down again

To days before the Internet
And Sunday trading laws
To days of If I show you mine
Will you show me yours

Bubble gum and Lucky bags
Runouts and Kiss Chase
Knock down Ginger,Tin can Tommy
The School Cross country race

Climbing over the closed park fence
Getting Conkers from the tree
Days when all "Those Bloody Kids"
Were Bloody, You and Me

School holidays and Bicycles
Staying out 'til it got dark
Red Rover tickets on London Buses
That took us to St. James's park

First Loves, School and Innocence
The mess from a Fountain pen
Oh to be a Kid again
Not now mind you... Back then

Slippers ...

I knew that I was getting old
when I looked in Marks's window
I saw a pair of slippers
and thought to myself, Hello

They look very comfy,
I should get myself a pair
I never have worn slippers
but I didn't seem to care

They were lined with sheepskin
and had a fur band on the top
And open backed a bit more like
a mule or a flip flop

Fashioned from the finest leather
and hand stitched all the way
I wouldn't know whether to put them on
or put them on display

I stood there gazing longingly
I must have looked a treat
Looking in the window
and then looking at my feet

I'm sure they'd suit me
and they'd save my feet from getting cold
Getting excited by a pair of slippers?
My God I'm getting old. ..

The Misbegotten Troubadour ...

The room was almost empty
save the guy against the bar
A beat up old fedora
and an old steel string guitar
A cigarette hung from his lips
a whiskey in his hand
A misbegotten troubadour
the last one of the band

He took the Gibson from its case
and put it on his knee
And tuned the strings from E to E
now absentmindedly
The cigarette got stubbed out
by his heel when it was done
The familiar sound of the Zippo wheel
then sparked another one

And when he sang, he sang the blues
as to the manor born
The cigarettes and whiskey left
his vocal chords half torn
But just enough to leave him with
a voice that brings the tears
To songs of love and lovers lost
and pain and passing years

....

....

His old guitar so battered now
could tell a tale it's own
Scored deep by plectra, through the years
is deep and rich of tone
Played by fingers with minds their own
and such dexterity
Man and guitar, as they say
in perfect harmony

The songs of B B King and Eric Clapton
reach our ears
They mirror all our lives and hopes
and also all our fears
The guitar chills us to the bone
with notes so pure and blue
His own songs hit us where we live
his lyrics are so true

The whiskey bottle empty now
the butts crushed on the floor
The blues man's set is over
and we've heard what we came for
He puts his guitar, in it's case
and pulls his hat down low
His collar up he leaves the room,
so ends another show

Spring ...

Spring is in the air today
Well, I say it's in the air
I dropped the bugger on the floor
And, Boing!...it bounced somewhere

Well that's the nature of a spring
They'll bounce for no good reason
I'm sorry, did you think I meant
The changing of the season?

Oh No, the winter hasn't yet..
..decided it will leave
Before it does they'll be an Ace or two..
..from up it's sleeve

Don't be mislead if in the sky
You see a splash of blue
You can bet that soon, another monsoon
Will come to an umbrella near you

So keep your wellie boots handy
And your Flip Flops and paraffin heater
I don't know what the weather will do
After all, I'm not a mind reader ...

But me, I'm going equipped with a brolly
If I can just fix this thing
Turn that to the right, Push this bit up tight
Now, Where is that flippin' spring ?.....

Seven Years Old ...

I used to love Gobstoppers,
Sherbet dips and lollies
Merry maids and Bazooka Joes,
Boiled sweets and toffees

Primary school, and playing out
Even when the weather got cold
Dirt and swings and roundabouts,
I used to be seven years old

Roller skates and hide and seek,
Playing knock down ginger
Splashing in puddles, getting words muddled
And egg chips and beans for my dinner

Playing football, three and in,
Eating Spanish Gold
Falling asleep in the back of Dad's car,
I used to be seven years old

But now it's Werther's Originals,
Rennies and Sugar free gum
Cough Candy, Liquorice and Newberry fruits
And Popcorn when the Grandchildren come

Falling asleep in front of the telly,
A hat and scarf when it gets cold
I don't get to play Kiss chase anymore
I wish I was seven years old....

I Remember ...

I remember the first time I did it
I remember the look on her face
I remember thinking the next morning
I could never go back to that place

I don't think it went how I planned it
I think it was over too soon
I don't think it lived up to her expectations
If I'm honest there wasn't much room

My moves were a little bit childish
My rhythm a little bit out
I could see that she was disappointed
And I soon guessed what that was about

I don't think it's totally my fault
And I'm not sure that I was to blame
It takes Two to Tango and she was the teacher
I never took a dance class again

The Early Morning Ninja ...

I woke up this morning, so the day started well
They don't start much better than that
As I opened my eyes, it was with some surprise
That I heard a strange noise, "What was that" ?

It sounded like somebody trying the back door
Someone was trying to break in
It's a strange time for burglars to be burgling I thought
Then my Ninja training kicked in

So, I leaped out of bed and ran for the stairs
Then I realised I was wearing no clothes
The element of surprise is one thing I thought
But I did feel a little exposed

Another noise, "Was that the window that time"?
By now I was forming a plan
Just then I remembered, I wasn't a Ninja
But a half naked, half asleep man

So I armed myself with a coat-hanger
I pulled back the curtain a ways
And there he was smiling and waving at me
Widow cleaners start early these days

Supermarket Shopping ...

I've just been down to the supermarket
Playing my favourite game
Looking in ev'ryones elses trolley
I wonder if you do the same

Looking at how many sweeties she's bought
And how many bottles of wine ?
Holier than thou, It's easy somehow
I hope they're not looking in mine

The woman ahead with the five loaves of bread
And the two bits of filleted trout
She must be feeding the five thousand
It's a miracle, I want to shout

And then there's the bloke with the full case of Coke
And eight bottles of sparkling water
When he leaves this shop, he might go off pop
And so will his son and his daughter

Of course there's the girl who's shopping for one
One onion, a cabbage, some beans and a plum
Foods that for all the effects are well known
Sometimes it's better folk's live on their own

But not me I'm healthy, it's salad and veg
And chicken and thinly sliced ham
Oh yes and a Pizza to put in the freezer
For emergencies you understand

But the Grandkids are coming around this weekend
So some chocolate and popcorn is fine ....
Oh look now at how many sweeties I've bought
And how many bottles of wine ?.....

The Country Singer ...

On the wall above the bar sits a beat up old guitar
And it looks as though it's seen much better days
Then an old guy wanders in and buys himself a glass of gin
And takes that old guitar down and he plays

He's thumbing and he's licking and he's strumming and he's picking
Then he settles on a sad old country song
It's one that we all know and he plays it kinda slow
So we sip our beer start to sing along

Then he plays a Willie Nelson song and we realise before too long
This guy is good but singing through his pain
He's seen and done it all before and like a million times or more
He's singing Blue eyes crying in the rain

He sits up on an old bar stool his tee shirt says that old guys rule
He sings just like an angel fell to earth
He drinks another gin and then familiar chords begin
And he's singing Country Roads for all he's worth

How do I live by Leanne Rimes, Kris Kristoferson's For the Good Times
He's singing ev'ry country song we know
Another gin is poured but just sits there most ignored
While he sings the Jim Reeves song He'll have to go

But now the show is over and as quickly as he came,
He slugs his gin and hangs that old guitar back up again
He leaves us with a thank you just for listening to his woes
Country music fans will know the way that feeling goes....

If I Ruled The World ...

If the Day ever dawns when I rule the world
You can bet your life It'll be a Tuesday
The day when nobody else really cares
Let's face it a bit of an Old News day

The working week starts on a Monday
A fact of which we're all aware
Wednesday as always is the middle of the week
So Tuesday's a bit of a spare

But if no-one else wants it I'll take it
I never look a gift horse in the mouth
So today then I am the King of the World
And tomorrow, It's back down to earth

But for now you can all do my bidding
And I won't ask for much that's for sure
Get something for free and bring it to me
I'll be in the pub until four

Please treat my day with respect and affection
And take my advice, be discreet
Keep your head above water, You're hand on your ha'penny
And never the twain shall meet

How Did Your Day Go ? ...

How did your day go?, did it go well?
Mine was a cracker a tale I'll now tell
It poured down with rain and I got soaking wet
I've been in for ages and ain't dried off yet

I had an umbrella but that was too small
It was obviously Mary's, it was stood by the wall
It also had two off the prongs sticking out
And the clip didn't fasten, I didn't half shout

Then it occurred why it was by the wall
It was headed for the dustbin and hadn't made it, that's all
I wish I'd have chucked it in the bin as I passed
For what good it was but I couldn't be arsed

I trod in a puddle while I walked for the bus
It soaked through my sock but I didn't make a fuss
But I did drop the brolly as my foot went right down
And thought I might catch it before it hit the ground

But unfortunately no, that just wasn't to be
My hand hit the floor then the brolly hit me
But I carried on Manfully, you know how you do
Making out nothing had happened to you

So onwards and upwards, the bus came along
I put down the umbrella but something was wrong
The Bus kept on going, It weren't the right one
But he splashed through the puddle, I guess just for fun

So there lies the story of how I got wet
Or is this story lies and I ain't been out yet?
Whatever the truth is, I'm not gonna tell
How did your day go?, did it go well?

Grandpa ...

Deep blue mountains disappear, in the milky mist
Dreams of chances long ago, casually missed
Long lost loves and long lost youth
All gone without a trace
Except the lines there to remind him
Deep etched in his face

The colours as the sun goes down cast shadows all around
Of red and amber, gold and blue, all patterned on the ground
The beauty takes his breath away, as ever it was so
His mem'ry takes him back again, to where he used to go

His life's been good, he knows that well, but now he's getting old
The summer sun is going down and now he's feeling cold
He wonders where the time has gone and did he use it well
His legacy's his family, and they'll have tales to tell

He's woken from his reverie, his melancholy gone
The sound of children's laughter brings him back from times bygone
The children screaming "Grandpa" as they run to the old man
He staggers from his chair and smiles as only Grandpa can

Pick us up and swing us round
Just like you always do
Little things please little children,
And sometimes big ones too

Marbles ...

Does anybody still have all their Marbles
Once they get past Fifty Eight or Nine?
'Cos up as far as Fifty eight, I thought that I was doing great
But then the whole thing went into decline

I can't remember where I put my whassname?
And what's that little orange thingy called?
Oh you know the thing I mean, that goes inside the Coffee machine
That we've had since the kitchen was installed

Now I know I left my Glasses on the table
I've looked for them but haven't found them yet
If I could find where they might be, I'd put them on so I could see
And look that thing up on the internet

Oh there they are, who put them on the armchair?
I'll clean them first then I'll have the last word
So, switch on the computer, and then the wireless router
And now I can't remember my password

Does anybody still have all their Marbles?
I'm sure I did once but I can't remember
Never mind what you may find, at Fifty Eight or Fifty Nine
I'll be Sixty flippin' One come next in December ...

A Spanish Sunday Morning ...

The coffee tastes good, well I knew that it would
I've sat here for breakfast before
The church bells are ringing, Sinatra is singing
And the whole town's beginning to stir

The women are dressed in their Sunday best
As they gather around the church square
The shops start to open, a small dog is barking
And the Sun splashes light everywhere

Ev'rything happens at Sundays pace
Nobody's rushing, it isn't a race
Just as another roller shutter goes up
The pretty girl pours me another hot cup

Blinds are pulled up and the Windows are opened
Sleepy heads take their first glance
Out on the terrace above the cafe
Somebody waters the plants

The streets are filling up slowly
There's a buzz of excitement about
Holidaymakers and photograph takers
And locals are all coming out

Does life ever get any better than this
A Sunday so fresh and pristine
I surely can't say but think I will stay
For just one more shot of caffeine

Flamenco ...

A minor chord came singing from the Six String On his lap
From somewhere in the darkness came a slow and rhythmic clap
A battered spotlight came to life, from just above the door
And sent a cone of pure white light onto the wooden floor.

The plaintiff cry that follows sends a shiver to your soul
The locals know it all too well, this song from long ago
We wait with bated breath because the Dancer's coming soon
And when she does her beauty sends a gasp around the room

Her dress is red as cherry, with polka dots of black
She wears it high around her neck and open down her back
The frills around the bottom swish and swirl as if there grown
She knows today, she's going to make, that wooden floor her own

The stamp of metal tips you think will surely split the floor
Before you know it, she has tapped, a hundred times or more
Her face set hard in concentration, for dancing is her life
The guitar player plays unseen, tonight's about his wife

His hair hangs down across his face, the sweat runs down his back
He watches as his strumming hand, puts the guitar under attack
Guitar and dance intensify, and reach crescendo pitch
The pounding rhythm, the pounding feet, you can't tell which is which

The clapping sound intensifies, it's coming to a close
She hadn't even noticed them, 'til one by one they rose
Then somewhere from the darkness, a lone voice calls Olé...
The crowd went wild, they'd seen a real Flamenco danced today

A Grand Day Out ...

From Beckton on the DLR, change at Canning Town
North Greenwich on the Jubilee, and back above the ground
The Riverbus along the Thames, pass the docklands towers
Getting off at London Bridge, avoiding April showers

Stroll through Borough Market, with it's sights and smells and sounds
Pass the old Clink prison and museum, back around
And out onto the South Bank, and left at the Anchor pub
Watch the guys canoe the Thames, from the local boating club

The sun's out now it's getting warmer, Spring has finally sprung
Ev'rybody's out today, just walking having fun
Tossing coins in a Busker's hat, and listening for a time
Walking on we sing that song, it's "This Old Heart Of Mine"

Passing the Globe theatre, William Shakespeare and all that
A guy on stilts in the stripey coat and the star spangled top hat
Stop and grab a bite to eat from the Indian street food stall
A nice cold Cobra beer, to wash it down and now we're full

Then on up to the London Eye with thousands having fun
Watching entertainers, or just sitting in the sun
We cross over the bridge to use Westminster Underground
And take the Jubilee line back and change at Canning Town

We're nearly home and knackered and there never was a doubt
That all in all, that really was...
A proper Grand Day Out...

Not Cool ...

I'm not as cool as I thought I was
I don't like the things cool people like
I wear Crocs and write verse and what seems to be worse
I wouldn't be caught dead on a bike

I never thought Spike Milligan was funny
And I was never a David Bowie Fan
And Springsteen's the Boss? ..I don't think so because...
...For Me Frank Sinatra's the Man

I like watching Rom Com's on telly.
And enjoy a Glass of Cheap Red Wine
Making Loom Bands with the Grandchildren
And the first Karaoke song's mine

For Me, James Dean films are depressing
And Bruce Lee makes Me want to swear
I'm not as cool as I thought I was
But d'you know what? I really don't care

If ...

If your get up and go, got up and went
If your spending money's already been spent
If your giving up stuff and it's not even Lent
Don't worry, you'll always have Me

If you notice, with time, that your waistline is growing
If you go for a walk and you're puffing and blowing
If you get all dressed up and you find your slip's showing
Don't worry. you'll always have Me

If your memory is not what it was anymore
If you've just gone upstairs and you don't know what for
If your eyesight can only be described as poor
Don't worry, You'll always have Me

If you find, more than ever, you're feeling the cold
If the story you're telling's already been told
If whatever you're selling's already been sold ...

You're on your own you old git

Brought up in the Fifties ...

My mate lived in a Prefab
Just across the Mile End Road
Another one lived in a little flat
That sometimes overflowed
We lived in a terraced house
That we shared with our Nan
Another family, my Step-dad knew,
Lived in a caravan

We never had much money,
But we were never poor
We had all we needed
And we had our own street door
So what our jeans weren't Levi's,
And our plimsolls weren't Green Flash
Free school dinners taste the same
If you haven't got the cash

Making do and mending
Were the tenets we lived by
It stood us in good stead and taught us,
You don't always have to buy
If it's broke then fix it,
Lessons that we learned and lost,
Lessons we could learn today,
Know the value not the cost

Brought up in the fifties,
A different time and space
A clip 'round the ear from a copper
And a bicycle without any brakes
No mobile phones or computers,
No personal panic alarm
Staying out late and No sell by dates ...
It didn't do us any harm ...

Scooter Boy ...

Back in nineteen seventy one,
we rode our scooters, just for fun
Up and down the Roman Road,
dressed In What Was A La Mode
Clean white Staypressed trousers
and checked Ben Sherman shirts
Sunglasses and a Parka
and the girls wore pop fronted skirts
We never wore a crash hat,
It wasn't yet the law
They didn't suit the image,
We were posers to the core

The soundtrack was all Motown,
Diana Ross and Marvin Gaye
Junior Walker, Jimmy Ruffin
Not forgetting Michael J
Stevie Wonder, Gladys Knight,
Smokey, all such fun
And don't forget that..
"Patches....I'm depending on you son"

My first bike was a Lambretta, an SX225
I fell off that one more than once
And lucky to survive
The roundabout at Vicky park
Will always spring to mind
It scares me now to think of it
But back then life was kind

....

....

Then came the SS180,
The Vespa I loved so much
My brother owned it before me
And it had a fearsome clutch
The front wheel lifted off the ground
As it pulled away
Good job there weren't much traffic then
And we're still here today

The "Quadrophenia" violence was,
By then, of long ago
It was all about the bikes and the girls,
Or we didn't want to know
Alas I have no photographs
To remind me of those days
Just the pictures in my head
And the games my memory plays
We were too cool for cameras
Or to stand still for that long
But let me say, right here, right now,
I'm sorry we were wrong

And then we got seduced by cars
As ev'ry one will know
A heater for the winter
And an Eight Track stereo
We missed the bikes the most of all
For days out in the sun
But nights in cars, as we all learned,
Brought a different kind of fun.

Life, Part One (The Dog)

It's tougher being a Dog than A Cat
Especially when you're getting old
She gets a sandbox in the corner of the kitchen
I have to go out in the cold

She sits on the sofa, licking her bits
And purring away with delight
Getting herself ready, she's going out soon
Where does she go every night

The one in the skirt tells the one in the trousers
Take that dog out for a walk
I don't want to go, It's looking like snow
But I'm told to shut up when I talk

Now I know that snow always looks nice
But with legs that are as short as mine
My dangly bits will get frozen
So I'll stay here if you don't mind

The box in the corner, with small people in
Is on and the Trousered one's swearing
Someone just scored and the Skirted one's bored
And I wonder why that cat is staring

The one in the trousers, took me to the vet
For... Believe Me, you don't want to know
Now I'm not vindictive, but if I catch him naked
Then His bits may just have to go

The Morning is here and the Biped's have gone
And Tiddles is sleeping like a log
But after today, I think you must say
That there's still life left in This Old Dog....

Life, Part Two (The Man)...

I'm very sorry about Yesterday,
I got up late and was having my bath
I understand my Dog was on here
And spoke to you on my behalf

Did he tell you a shaggy dog story
'cos he really thinks that he's funny
I don't let him put his stuff on here much
He'll be asking for half of the Money

I swear that dog's getting past it
And losing some doggie brain power
You should see the way that he looks at Me
When he sees me step out of the Shower

And when I'm watching the football
And outside it's cold and it's dark
He wants to go out,leaves me in no doubt
And to let me know, He'll sit and bark

Even when it's snowing outside
He for some reason still wants to go
Mind you I laugh when I turn around
And see the drag marks in the Snow

And as for the Cat, Don't start me on that
Why is that thing always staring?
She looks at me while I'm watching the footie
I think she objects to the swearing

And as for the wife, The light of my life
She likes to keep me on my toes
Why do I keep a dog and still Bark myself
'Cos her and the cat don't I suppose....

Life, Part Three (The Cat)...

Okay, If I must then I'll tell you
Of the joys that my life here can bring
You've all read the story from my Pet Man,
And also you've heard from ...That Thing

So what, I go out in the evening?
But what is a girl going to do
If you had the chance to go out and dance
I'm sure you would jump at it too

The Thing often wonders where I go at Night
And trust Me if only he knew
But if I were to tell him, He can't keep a secret
And I know he'd end up telling you

The day that the Thing came home from the vet
And was limping, I laughed 'til I cried
His Boys had been nicked and his bark was high pitched
And he couldn't catch me if he tried

And then they accuse me of staring
Staring at them ?, Pish and Tosh
If only they knew, I'm staring right through them
While I give myself a dry wash

Then there's the smells, well don't get me started
While most of them come from the Thing
They can't all be him and to judge by his grin
The Man gets his two pennyworth in

....

....

So I sit and I clean and I stretch and i preen
And I sharpen my claws on his chair
The woman's okay and I sit on her lap
And pretend that the others aren't there

The strange thing with both of the people
Is they think that i am their Pet
They Feed and they keep me, I do what I like
There's Irony here they don't get.......

Well, It's Saturday now and I've looked out the window
And it looks like its going to rain
So keep yourself dry and keep your Paws clean
For tonight we go hunting again

Fish and Chips ...

You can't beat a nice plate of Fish and Chips
Whenever you're down at the coast
With the salt, sea air and the sand in my hair
It's the thing I look forward to most

A nice bit of Haddock, or a Beer Battered Cod
With Chips, and Baked Beans for that matter
A nice pot of Tea and I'm sure you'll agree
Two slices of bread with real butter

Now that's what I call real seaside food
Not Sausage, or Burger and Fries
Get some real Fish and Chips, from your plate to your lips
It's a pleasure you cannot disguise

So next time you're there and the kids say they're hungry
Don't just take them in some Maccy D's
Get them a nice plate of Fish, Chips and Beans
Or if you're Northern they can have Mushy Peas

Dead Phone ...

Well, my Smart-phone isn't so smart anymore
In fact it's dumber than Me
At least I know how to work in the mornings
To a greater or lesser degree

But I've pressed all the buttons it just won't come on
I've Stared at it, Glared at it, Lord knows what's wrong
I've plugged it back in but the battery's strong
I think it is now an Ex phone

Not to be confused with an X Box
Which I believe is something totally other
I've even tried swearing and giving it a "Tap"
But I don't think it's going to recover

So I won't be on Facebook at all today
'Til my working day has come and gone
Do you think I should put my phone in my pocket
In case it decides to come on ?

But there's good news, they're going to replace it
And the new one will be here tonight
Just in time for my holiday tomorrow,
Did I mention? ....I did ? .. Oh that's right..

So today I'll be incommunicado
And tomorrow I'll be in Spain
So have a good day, hold on don't go away
I'll just try the phone once again .....

Dieting ...

I've gone on a bit of a diet,
About time I hear some of you say
It's got to the stage where, to quote Chas and Dave,
My beer belly gets in my way

But it's not beer, it's food that has caused it
And biscuits and chocolate and wine
And sweeties and peanuts and crisps and cake,
And other bad habits of mine

I'd like to lose maybe a couple of stone
And you never can tell, I just might
But I'd have to admit that I cheated a bit
'cos we did have a Chinese last night

But I don't think the diet alone's gonna do it
To get me the shape that I'd like
I may have to do the unthinkable thing
I may have to get me a bike

But I promise I'll stick to the parks and byways
And I'll do it in shorts and tee shirt
Can you imagine seeing me wearing Lycra?
I don't want to cause you that hurt

Or maybe I'll go out and run to get fit
I'll think about that for a while
Or perhaps I could get me a Gym membership
There now, that's made you all smile

I'm sure one of the above is the answer
But the thought of it makes me all jumpy
This dieting's not all it's cracked up to be
To be honest, It just makes me Hungry ...

Doing Nothing ...

You know when you're laying out in the hot sun
And you feel your skin starting to tingle
You're drifting away and all thoughts of today
And tomorrow are starting to mingle

You're not quite asleep but you're feeling it creep
'Round the edges of your conscious mind
You're losing the fight and realise you might
Soon drop off and you suddenly find...

You're sound asleep now but strangely somehow
You're aware of the heat from the sun
You drift in and out then you hear someone shout
But it's only some kids having fun

You come back to the stage of "Where am I"
But you know that you don't really care
The birds are still singing, the sky is still blue
And that warm summer sun is still there

Well, they are the times we remember
The days that are good for our soul
Days we will treasure, days of simple pleasure
Doing nothing's the new Rock and Roll

Dublin ...

Strolling round the streets of Dublin after thirty some odd years
Nothing seems familiar then a memory appears
Bewley's down on Grafton St, St Stephens Green, The Quays
Slattery's in Capel St., It all comes back to me.

The drunken nights, the Guinness in us, The Music and the Craic
It's changed, We've changed, Life goes on, I guess you can't go back
Then someone chimes "The Rare Auld Times" , My favourite Dublin song
We raise a glass to times gone past And we all sing along

I remember Dublin City, Well at least that's what I thought
But old ways must make way for new, it's what we're always taught
And there's a statue, Is that new? The infamous Molly Malone
Her wheelbarrow all but empty now Save raindrops splashed on stone

Round Temple Bar, where the tourists are, With Restaurants, Clubs and Bars
And then up to O'Connell street where the Spike reaches up to the Stars
The Beckett Bridge that spans the Liffey and looks like a laid down Harp
The 02 Stadium, The Financial zone all clean and bright and sharp

But I couldn't find the Dublin, That I loved in Memory
Perhaps I found the real one and the change had been in me
It's still a vibrant City and it buzzes night and day
It's young and brash and maybe it has always been that way

East End Pubs ...

The East End pub of myth and legend, will never reappear
Singing songs 'round the old piano, while balancing your beer
Sally Sally, pride of our alley, and Make yourself at home
Nelly Dean and Muvver Brown, Over land or sea or foam

And then we all got affluent and hey they got a band
Some of them now household names but here they made their stand
Some pubs went down the mellow route and some set out to shock
Some pubs went for cabaret and some for solid rock

Then the strippers came and went, it was just a bit of fun
Until the breath test came along and we knew we were done
The pubs still had their last hurrah when Disco came along
And we all knew the words to ev'ry Michael Jackson song

We'd cram in, standing cheek by jowl and all become one crowd
We couldn't hear what anyone said, the music was so loud
Shouting to each other, and smoking cigarettes
Drinking too much alcohol but having no regrets

But now it's gone full circle and we now look for a seat
And someone tickles the ivories, while we sit down and eat
The East End pub of myth and legend, may never reappear
But the people get what the people want, and that's what we have here...

Sick Car ...

My car has gone into hospital
It's making a funny noise
At the moment I'm legging it everywhere
And trust me, that isn't by choice

I've just walked back from Canning Town
And it took me three quarters of an hour
But now I'm back in and the very first thing
Is to go back upstairs for a shower

Then after my shower, a nice cup of tea
And maybe a biscuit or two
Some Crunchy Nut Corn Flakes, a second cup of tea
And I'll drop this quick message to you

I'm meant to be playing Golf today
But I can't take my clubs on a bus
I don't think my Bus Pass will cover us both
And you know someone will make a fuss

Well anyway that's all I've got for today
So I don't think I'll be going far
Just maybe as far as the greeting card shop
For a Get Well Soon card for my car ...xx

Everyone I've Been ...

An ode to everyone I've been and those I'm yet to know
To all the places that I've seen and where I'm still to go
To all the jokes I've ever told and all those that I've heard
To all the songs that I have sung and to the spoken word

To being young and growing old, to loving Hot and liking cold
To laying in the sun again and then to walking in the rain
To family, work rest and play, to staying home and to going away
Regrets and triumphs, both the same, taking credit accepting blame

Living, Loving, Laughing, Crying, Mostly winning, always trying
Never rich but never poor, Always with my own street door
A lifetime blessed from birth to now, Nigh sixty years and still somehow...
It's all in front and all behind, and age is just a state of mind

Life's been good and Life is good and even getting better
I read this note that I just wrote as if it was a letter...
To everyone I've been before and those I'm yet to know
One thing's for sure, I want some more, let's get on with the show...

The Circus ...

Roll up, Roll up, the Ringmaster called,
the circus is coming to town
Alright, we haven't got Elephants,
and the Lions have all gone to ground
We don't have a bearded lady either,
Immac took good care of that
But we do have a bloke who's got a moustache
and he's got an old Tabby cat

The letter from Health and Safety said
our High Wire must get lower
And the bloke who rode the Wall of Death,
had to ride much slower
Those daring young men on the Flying Trapeze
had to clip their wings
And the show's now over, long before,
the fuller figured lady sings

The Clown's car failed it's M.O.T.,
and so that's the end of that
And the girl who rode the ponies around,
didn't wear a hard hat
It also turned out that the sawdust was toxic,
so of course that had to go
Then the bloke, from the local council,
came 'round to watch the show

It seems we had the wrong permit,
so the human cannonball couldn't fire
And throwing a bucket of cut up paper,
made everybody perspire
Roll up, Roll up, the Ringmaster called,
the circus is coming to town
It's not quite the same as it used to be ...
But they still have that scary arsed clown

Kids Games ...

Swinging from the lampost at the corner of your street
Splashing through the puddles, with nothing on your feet
Three and in or Next Goal wins,
Can we have our ball back please
Run outs, Kiss Chase, Knock Down Ginger,
we played them all with ease

Penny Up The Wall, Tin Can Tommy,
The rules changed every day
We don't play it like that anymore,
we'd found a whole new way
Skipping Ropes and Jacko Skates
and a Cart held together with twine
Wheels from a pram and an Orange box
and anything else we could find

Cowboys and Indians, Building a camp,
Playing out 'til it was dark
In the winter we'd play in the street where we lived,
In the summer we'd go to the park
Bouncing a ball, first the floor then the wall,
then catching and throwing again
Drawing a wicket for a quick game of Cricket,
washed off when it started to rain

Kiss Chase, Jacks, and Coloured Chalk,
Catapults and Dinky Toys,
Dolls and Prams for little girls Girls,
Cars and Guns for boys
Trikes and Bikes and scooters
and the DING of a bicycle bell
What happened to when I was young?
I remember it all so well ....

I Don't Believe in Astrology ...

I don't believe in Astrology
But I read in the paper today
That because I'm a Sagittariun Male
Something was coming my way

Now, it wasn't very specific
About what it was, why or when
But it sounded as if I would like it
So I quickly read through it again

It seems that the Moon's in My Ascendant
To be honest I didn't feel a thing
But now that I know, I hope it don't show
It's a little bit embarrassing..

Does anyone know where my Ascendant is?
And if you do what does it do?
I hear that Aquarians let the sun shine in
Does that mean that they have one too ?

You're never alone with a Gemini
And Libra will balance the scales
The Pisces will swim when the Crab lets them in
And Scorpios have a sting in the tail

All Taureans evidently talk Bull
And the Leo will always chase Aries
Virgo's aren't kidding anyone
And Capricorns away with the fairies

So anyway, I'm sitting here waiting
Maybe this time next year we'll be rich
I don't believe in astrology
But my Ascendant's started to itch ....

Fashions ...

"Surely you're not going out like that",
I remember my Mum said to me
And then I said it, and my Son said it,
On and back through eternity

"At least tuck your shirt in", or "those jeans are dirty",
or the classic, "Have you got your coat"?
"They said it might rain", and then came the refrain,
who are They ? and who cares what they wrote

Youngsters will wear what youngsters will wear
And as grown ups we don't understand
Jeans at half mast, shoes that don't last and
"Vintage", to us? Second hand

But why would we want to stop them
With their caps on the wrong way around
Remember that we wore Platform Shoes
And stood about a a foot off the ground

Bell Bottom trousers when I was a kid
And bleaching your Levi's in patches
Big collared shirts and girls in suede skirts
And colours that nobody matches

I remember I once had a pair of old jeans,
That I had cut off at the knee
"Surely you're not going out like that",
I remember my Mum said to me

Christmas ...

The temperature is dropping, It's December after all
Christmas time is coming, do you think the snow will fall
Carol singers at your door with songs of Holy Night
To Celebrate the Son of God, We never should lose sight

Tinsel, Balls and Christmas Trees And lights of red and green
The Shops are filling up with all things Christmas once again
Their shelves weighed down and baskets bulging, Gifts for girls and boys
Festive songs from every shop, a cacophony of noise

Santa Claus is on his way, The elves work now is done
Naughty or nice, the list is his and now he has his fun
On Christmas Eve All Girls and Boys try hard to stay awake
To hear sleigh bells and reindeer rattle over their roof slates

Oh little town of Bethlehem , let Love and joy abound
Brass bands playing in the street a real uplifting sound
The Holly and the Ivy, the wreath on your front door
Let's rejoice Our favourite season comes around once more

Be good to one another and spread happiness and joy
Smile just for the sake of it, help someone else enjoy
The time it seems that ev'rybody else is having fun
Happy day's, Peaceful Nights.... Merry Christmas Everyone

A Ray Of Hope ...

It started on a night like this
two thousand years now gone
In the dark and Midnight sky
a brand new bright star shone
Those who saw it followed it
for they knew where it lead
To Bethlehem, a manger
where a baby lay his head

An infant child was born to us
to take away our sins
The weight of the world placed on his shoulders
The light of the world within
It's Christmas eve we celebrate
the birth of our salvation
Let's not forget the reason for
this season's incarnation

I believe, if we believe
we'll find the peace inside
And love of life will follow
when we get ourselves onside
The child became man and sacrificed
ev'rything for you
Be nice to people in his name
it's the least that you can do

Christmas Fayre ...

Christmas is coming but I'm not ready yet
I'm sure that I've still got more shopping to get
The cupboards are filling with good festive fayre
But there are still some things I'm sure that aren't there

I've got, Chocolate Brazil Nuts, Twiglets and Cheese
Pickled Red Cabbage and a bag of frozen Peas
Silverskin Onions and Mixed Fruit and Nuts
Gherkins for Boxing day to go with Cold Cuts

A Large Tin of Roses and some Quality Street
Two Frozen Turkeys with Giblets complete
A big bag of Chestnuts and Cranberry sauce
A packet of Dates and a Pudding of course

An extra large box of After Eight Mints
Newberry Fruits that are fit for a Prince
A box of Matchmakers, the orange ones I love
And Oh yes, that's right, another box of the above

The Veggies and 'Taters, of course I'll get fresh
Carrots and Parsnips and Sprouts in a mesh
Though I'm sure there is something I haven't yet got
I just can't remember what I have forgot ....

Christmas Eve ...

Well here it is then it's Christmas Eve.
Let the fun and festivities commence
After you've finished with work that is
And been out and bought the last presents

Then a small glass of sherry to get you quite merry
And a mince pie should set you off right
But don't eat too many 'cos there won't be any
To pick at on the sofa tonight

Is your Turkey out of the freezer ?
Have your Brussels Sprouts been peeled and crossed
Are you sure you've enough of the cranberry stuff
And how much did those Onions cost?

An early night, now that's what's called for
To prepare yourself for the big day
Well, maybe a beer to bring you good cheer
And another to help it on its way

There must be a film on.. " It's a Wonderful Life "
My favourite, I'll stay up for that
I'll just open that tin of Quality Street
And throw the wrappers at the Cat

But sooner or later I must go to bed
I need to be fresh in the morning
I can't greet my guests in their Sunday best
And sit at the dinner table yawning

But that's all for later, let's get on with now
And start the day off with a smile
Be young, Be foolish, Be Dame Edna Everage
You'll find it'll all be worthwhile

Christmas Morning ...

Well, here it is the day of days,
The Twenty Fifth of December
Wrapping Paper everywhere
and Children trying to remember
Who bought me this? What does that do?
and Where's my money gone
Dad sitting there in his new Pyjamas
while Mum gets the Brussels Sprouts on

What time did you tell your Dad to come round?
Mum calls through the Kitchen door
I said about Twelve, for Dinner at Two,
Dad says but he's not really sure
The Christmas CD is on and it's playing
the songs that we all know and Love
Apart from the one that they always put on them
by someone you've never heard of

The noise level rises as more big surprises
are opened from under the tree
Be careful.. Don't do that .. Oh, who knocked that over
and who's is this Blur DVD?
D'you think it's to early for a small glass of Sherry?
Mum says as the morning tea's done
She wanders back to the kitchen
to see how the Sprouts are getting on

....

....

It's time for the Turkey to go in the oven
It's bigger than usual this year
This is when Dad comes into his own,
I'll do that, no, just give me that here
It's a sixteen pound bird and somewhere he's heard
that you cook twenty minutes per pound
And add twenty minutes without the tin foil
It comes out a nice Golden Brown

Mum goes and sits down in her new dressing gown
and a spritz of Chanel number five
A Family day in the old fashioned way
Then someone pulls into the Drive
A panic attack .. Oh No who is that?,
Dad runs and looks out to be sure
The car then backs out, they made a mistake,
They're visiting Molly next door

Christmas Morning, a day like no other a day
where nothing has been overlooked
It all goes so well, except for the Brussels,
as usual they'll be undercooked
There'll be eating and drinking with Family and Friends
the Holiday has just begun
I'll say Merry Christmas and like Tiny Tim said...
God Bless us Everyone

Christmas Night ...

Christmas Night, our guests have gone
and everything is put away
We're sitting in front of the television
reflecting on our perfect day
A turkey sandwich and a glass of red wine
and as I just said to the wife
In the immortal words of my favourite movie...
"It's a Wonderful Life"

I feel like I've put on a stone and a half
and really must stop eating soon
I'll just have one more Mince pie and custard
but perhaps use a much smaller spoon
The After Eight mints were all gone before six
and the mixed nuts have gone the same way
There isn't much left of the Christmas Cake
and the wine HAD a lovely bouquet

But the lights are down low and we've nowhere to go and
"Love Actually" is just coming on
We'll sit here and doze and then I suppose
put the kettle on for tea before long
I hope that your day went much the same way
and you're warm on the inside and out
Merry Christmas to you and those you love too ...
I should have passed on that last Brussels Sprout ....

Goodnight, God Bless ...

Into the arms of Morpheus, the God of sleep and dreams
Slipping into slumber with unconscious will it seems
The Sandman's done his job and sprinkled sleep dust in our eyes
It's time to face the certainty of one more days demise

Sleep the sleep of children, unconcerned and free from woe
Unleash your dreams and follow them wherever they may go
Close your eyes and climb aboard the Morningtown Express
Tomorrow will come soon enough, We gave this day our best

Siesta, Snooze or Shuteye, Forty Winks or in a Trance
Catnap, Doze or in Repose we all grab every chance
But when it comes to Nigh time as into out beds we creep
We know there's nothing that compares to a proper good nights sleep

I'll say Rest well to everyone and hope sleep comes your way
And if you dream of fame and fortune, That that comes too someday
Or if Peace and Love going hand in glove for you will mean success
I'll say to you and mean it true , My Friends, Goodnight God Bless

Fit or Fat ...

Sit down while I tell you a story
It's About a day in the life
Of someone who we, are gonna call Me
And Someone else I call my Wife

We'll start with the story of Mary
Who's already gone to the Gym
She goes ev'ry morning around about Dawning
That's how we both stay so slim

Now when I say both it's an aggregate
A bit like a joint Bank account
She works out and, drops a couple of pounds
And I put on two,.. It don't count

She says I should join her there one day
I'd love it, She tells me with glee
I don't know 'bout that, 'cos some of this fat
Well it's almost become part of me

By now you can see, that The Story of Me
And my Wife's, One of light and of dark
She treats her body just like it's a Temple
And mine's more a Disneyland Park

So ends today's little story
A story of fitness and health
A story of life, Of Me and my wife
And you also may recognise yourself .....

Faded Photos ...

The faded photo's tell a tale of 1950's life
Of times confined to history with their struggles and their strife
Of cobbled streets and horse drawn carts and fog, and yet somehow
We'd sooner be back there and then instead of here and now

The pictures show a simpler life to which we all aspire
Of Mums and Dads, of Sunday tea and sitting 'round the fire
The coach trips to the seaside, the parties in the street
Kids out playing football wearing nothing on their feet

Old tin baths and mangles nailed up out in the back yard
Outside toilets, cleaning doorsteps, cooking using Lard
The pub up on the corner with the scruffy public bar
Men in suits with pints of beer and your dad's old two tone car

We look back fondly to a time when Elvis was a lad
When Radio and Cinema were all the "tech" we had
No computers, Mobile Phones or Satellite TV
Why did they invent this stuff if not for you and me?

We got what we wanted, not what we needed, whether we knew it or not
And now look at us, we have everything but maybe we have lost the plot
You can't put the genie back in the bottle or turn back the hands of time
But we can get your photo's out once in a while
and remember us, back in our prime.....

Cockney ...

If you ever sat and watched
the sun go down from Southend Beach
And saw the cargo ships
sail up and down the Limehouse reach
If you ever sung two drunken verses
of Knees up Muvva Brown
Or sat in the traffic for ages and waited,
for the Blue Bridge to come back down

If you ever caught the District Line
from Mile End to Upton Park
Or cycled through the foot tunnel
to Greenwich and home before dark
If you went down the Roman on Saturday,
with Kelly's your restaurant of choice
And legged it back over the fence over Vicky,
when you heard the park keepers voice

If your house had an outside toilet,
that froze for three months of the year
And your Street had a Pub on the corner,
and that's where you had your first beer
If your Mum and Aunt Sally, danced up the Bow Palais,
while dodging the bombs going home
And you remember the days before "Tower Hamlets"
when the boroughs all stood on their own

Then the chances are you are a Cockney,
at least that is now how we're known
We never did hear the Great Bell of Bow
but the Bells of Bow Church are our own
The Docks may be gone but the plumbing's moved on,
and they knocked down the Odeon too
But when all's said and done, we were part of the fun,
and the East End still has Me and You

The Battle of Britain ...

Today we remember the Battle of Britain
And as ever remember the few
It's hard to imagine just what might have happened
Without what they went on to do

Vastly outnumbered in both man and machine
But never in guile or in spirit
The RAF pilots, both British and allied
Flew up to and over their limits

With an average age of around twenty two
And some were as young as Eighteen
Defending our Islands against the Great Foe
That most of them had never seen

Messerschmidt, Spitfires, Hurricanes and such
In pitched battles fought just overhead
And as ever in war, when it came to take score
Too many young men were dead

But the Battle was won and the enemy vanquished
By these brave men who did what we asked
Remember with pride those who fought and who died
Heroes right up to the last

Brick Lane ...

Brick Lane on a Sunday Morn.,
All human life is there
From New Age Hippies, through Old Age Yuppies
To girls with dyed green hair

From Bangla Town to the Beigel Shop
And Blackman's in Cheshire Street
Down Brick Lane on a Sunday
You'd be surprised who you might meet

East End faces in very strange places
West End Girls in there too
Wannabes, used to be's and those that never were
And people just like me and you

Buskers singing songs that make you sing along
Songs we knew before these kids were born
Artists and shoppers, Poets and coppers
Mothers and Lovers forlorn

Those there in search of a future
Those there to look for their past
Winers and diners, a crowd of Old Timers
And that girl from the Eastenders cast

It's all very different from when I was a nipper,
But really it's all still the same
Only the names and faces have changed
On a Sunday Morn. down in Brick Lane

Garden Gnomes ...

Did you ever wonder what life must be like
Lived as a Garden Gnome?
Do they sit there in the garden all day,
Even when no-one's at home?

Or do they go off, out with their mates,
Fishing a lake somewhere else
Bored with never catching that goldfish
That you put in your pond yourself

Maybe they'd go to a football match
And cheer on their favourites, West Ham
The one with the beard says he played for them once
But the others think that's just a scam

Then off to the pub for beer and a sing song
"Over land or sea or foam.."
A quick Pie and Mash and making a dash
For the bus 'cos it's time to go home

Home in the garden before you arrive
Sitting up on the toadstool
Line in the pond, beside the fern frond
While you suspect nothing at all

Or maybe they do, just sit there all day
And do nothing but stare into space
But can you be sure, when you go on your tour
That you left them right there in that place ?...

Old Friends and Remember Whens ...

Sitting with an old Guitar and two or three old friends
Messing with a few old tunes and a few remember whens
Singing the songs we used to sing though the high notes aren't the same
Smiling when we're missing them, the years can take the blame

Laughing about the old days when we'd pass the cigarette 'round
And strangely, how that strange aroma, would improve our sound
There's nothing there to help us now, the cigarettes have gone
And the whiskey's turned to coffee now that time and we've moved on

Singing "Seven Spanish Angels", just like Willie and Ray
"Crazy", "I've just seen a face" and "That'll be the day"
Well worn friends and well worn songs and well worn old guitars
Country songs and Sing alongs and Blues played in twelve bars

Jokes are told and the coffee goes cold and someone pours the Red Wine?
Then I carelessly strum a G and a D and an old Neil Young song comes to mind
"Harvest Moon", Oh what a tune, Can anyone still sing that high ?
At this stage nobody cares anymore so we may as well give it a try

There's time for one more cup of coffee, we've emptied the bottle of wine
Unplugged "Layla" rears it's head then someone mentions the time
It's now what we used to call early, but I know I'm no longer eighteen
Then "Last Saturday Night I Got Married".. , Yep, it's time for "Goodnight Irene"

A Day at the Seaside ...

A nice bracing walk around Brighton today
The sea breeze was blowing the cobwebs away
The waves crashing in made the loose pebbles roar
Spreading the foam all along the sea shore

Well, I got a bit peckish, you know how you do
So I opened some sweeties to have one or two
I finished them both and then two became three
As we leaned on the railings and looked at the sea

After the sweeties, we had Fish and Chips,
Some Tea and two slices of bread
In the Motorway services, we got Pick and Mix
And this time had Coffee instead

But a Chocolate Brazil can make you feel ill
Unless you have three or four more
I wish that I'd left the Chocolate Raisins alone
They've made me feel rough to the core

Now the diet's gone out of the window now
With all that I've eat this weekend
Now I can look forward to Monday
To start the whole thing off again

Perhaps I've undone, all the good that I'd done
But as always, remain a believer
Regrets are like Hairnets, for blokes who are Bald
And I have no use for them either

On Reflection ...

My bathroom mirror is haunted, an old bloke lives in there
With grey/white whiskers, baggy skin and fast receding hair
I wonder what the wife must think when she looks at his face
And does he frighten the Grandkids
when they stay at Grandad's place ?

He looks a bit like my old Dad
And a bit like the late Mike Read
He seems like he's been eating well,
He's fatter than me indeed

His eyes are sometimes bloodshot,
Like he stayed up late at night
Now when I get up to go for a wee,
I don't turn on the light

He blocks out my reflection
And he copies what I do
When I Shave and clean my teeth
He does the same things too

He's getting on my nerves a little bit
But here's the rub
He seems to look much younger
When I come in from the pub

I think I need a new mirror,
Or maybe I need a new face
A nip and a tuck and a squirt of Botox
To put a few things back in place

No seriously, that cannot be me,
It's the mirror that gives me a scare
Do me a favour, when you go in my bathroom,
See if you too see him there ...

I Never Learned to Dance ...

I've been a lot of places and I've seen a lot of stuff
Been up and down life's peaks and troughs, and in and out of love
But one regret I have in life, I never took the chance
I never stepped out on the floor,
I never learned to dance

I sing and play guitar a bit and tell a joke or two
I take a decent photograph and write in verse for you
I've learned a couple of things in life about lovin' and romance, but. .
I should have stepped out on the floor,
I should have learned to dance

Two left feet or so they say or just too shy to try
Leaning on the wall until someone would catch my eye
Snapping fingers shuffling feet then someone looks askance
I would have stepped out on the floor,
I would have learned to dance

The music stirs my very soul my body comes alive
I love the Waltz, the Tango and the Hustle and the Jive
I watch the dancers spinning with a slightly wistful glance
I could have stepped out on the floor,
I could have learned to dance

It's too late now my body doesn't do as it is told
My bones and joints are aching as I gracefully grow old
I'll hold on tight and shuffle if I have to make a stance ... but
I wish I'd stepped out on the floor,
I wish I'd learned to dance ...

Who are They?...

They covered up the cobbled stone
that ran along our street
They covered it with tarmac
that would melt in summer heat
Then they painted yellow lines along
so nobody could park
There weren't that many cars around ,
not even after dark

Then They pulled our houses down
and cancelled Watch with Mother
Moved us into blocks of flats,
One on top of the other
They took our shillings and pennies away
and gave us ten tens to the pound
Then called a Marathon Snickers,
They turned our whole world around

They'd taken Fred Barker, off of the Telly,
and even Ollie Beak
Pussy Cat Willum and Andy Pandy,
Yesterdays men so to speak
Then They decided, that we didn't need,
free school milk every day
So just like the Horse troughs, that we used to play in,
They just took the whole lot away

So with peanut Treets, now called M&M's,
and Opal Fruits are Starburst
Red Rover bus tickets, now part of history,
and advice always being reversed
They tell us that things aren't good for us,
and we'll be better off by far
But the worst thing is, when they've done all this,
We still don't know who They are ....

What If ? ...

What if the world were a little younger,
And by virtue of that so were we
What if I were, again Twenty Seven
And you were again Twenty Three

What if I had more hair than I have
And possibly slightly less waist
And your hair was maybe more Pepper than Salt
And you wore more Silk and less Lace

What if our past was in front of us
And we had it all still to come
If most of our future wasn't behind us
And our race wasn't so nearly run

But then, What if the sun shone at midnight
And what if what's yours wasn't mine
The way of the world is the way that it is
Everything in it's own time

Youth by it's nature is passing
And I'm glad that I passed mine with you
If it wasn't for us getting older together
Tell me what else would I do...

Tread Gently ...

Tread gently as you walk along
the street of broken dreams
Sometimes things are closer to the edge
than first it seems
Be careful where you place your tread
for somewhere lay my heart
I've loved you for a million years
and you have yet to start

You've never even noticed me
and now at last we meet
And when you smile and say hello
again I skip a beat
Broken hearts and brand new starts,
not always hand in hand
Words unsaid and smiles unread
still hard to understand

I know some day, I'll find a way
to tell you how I feel
But until then I'll smile again
and for a while conceal
That I love you, with all my heart,
and all that that can mean
Tread gently as you walk along
the street of broken dreams

Someone Else ...

This Morning, as I made the bed,
a random thought popped in my head
What if I was someone else somehow

What if I was the King of Spain,
or Ringo Starr or Michael Caine
I wonder what I would be doing now ?

I'd be off somewhere with never a care,
maybe on the South coast of France
or in a casino in old Monte Carlo
playing a quick game of chance

Or off to the palace, for tea with the Queen
and various Very I.P's
Or out on a yacht, showing off what I'd got,
while collecting my royalty fees

And then it occurred that if I was being was them,
then who was going to be Me?
Nicholas Cage? David Beckham
Or His Lordship from Downton Abbey?

I can't see Mary putting up with that,
but I won't put the thought in her head
so when I've finished, drinking my tea,
I'll carry on making the Bed

The Toothbrush ...

Now, I use a rechargeable toothbrush
With the push on replaceable head
And I'm gonna tell you what happened this morning
When I got up out of my bed

I went in the bathroom, to shower and shave
And as I put my razor away
I just caught the toothbrush with the head of the razor
And thus sent the thing on it's way

It fell from the bathroom cabinet
As I swung at it, trying to catch
But I just scraped my finger on the edge of the tap
And ended up with a small scratch

Well anyway it bounced off the sink with a "Ting"
And on to the top of the cistern
That's lucky I thought, It could have been worse
And it was 'cos there's more to be written

Of course it bounced, just one more time
And into the lavatory pan
I stood there and stared, just a little bit scared
To go delving down there with my hand

Now, as luck would have it, I'd just cleaned the toilet
But the pan was still covered in bleach
I looked through the milky, bleachy water
And there it was, just within reach

So the time came to make a decision
While I'm staring down in disbelief
So that why I'm in Asda, at this time in the morning
Without having yet cleaned my teeth

The Loft ...

I haven't been up in the loft for a while
So I thought I'd go up there today
Just to have a bit of a clear out
And maybe throw some stuff away

It's a little bit tight and there isn't much room
But I managed to get in and see
And the first thing I found, right there on the ground
Was the fairy off the old Christmas tree

There was a box full of old cups and saucers
Some knives, forks and spoons in a tray
Why did I put them up there in the first place
Why didn't I just throw them away?

There's an old picture frame but it isn't the same
'cos it's chipped and the glass has a crack
There's an old Snooker Cue and a Candlewick bedspread
By the wall over there at the back

There are boxes of Christmas decorations
And another box of bulbs just for spares
And the end of an old roll of carpet
That we used to have on the stairs

There's an old wooden crutch that wasn't used that much
But I really can't throw it away
I think I'll go down for a nice cup of tea
And attack this lot some other day ...

The Isle of Dogs ...

The Isle Of Dogs in E14 still stirs my memory
I lived there for a little while in 1973
No, actually it was later. 'Cos by then my son had arrived
But I knew it wouldn't rhyme if I'd said 1975

We lived in Kelson House, one of the councils tower blocks
And this was in the day's when we still had the London docks
The blue bridge was a nightmare, always going up and down
Ev'ry time the giant ships came sailing into town

The 277 was the only transport, unless you had a car
Remember, this was long before they built the DLR
I watched The London Arena built, and knocked down in it's prime
I wonder now, if they knew then, would they give it more time

But even long ago, before all this, when we were tykes
We'd cycle over there and through the tunnel on our bikes
We'd ride to Island Gardens, and then down i n the lift
And tell the bloke we'd push them through, I know you get my drift

We'd then come up at Greenwich and around The Cutty Sark
And back down through the tunnel to the island before dark
Some kids from my old school lived on the island way back then
Sometimes I'd go to say hello before cycling home again

It's all changed now, Canary Wharf now dominates the place
I love the way they've done it and I love the use of space
I know there are detractors and I understand their pain
But nothing we can say will ever change it back again

So celebrate The Isle Of Dogs, it's concrete glass and steel
Billingsgate and old dock cranes, all standing toe to heel
Manhattan Island on the Thames, down in our East End
'Cos ev'rybody knows the place, where the mighty river bends

The Hat ...

I left my new hat in Orlando
And together we'd been through a lot
I wore it that night that it rained down in Georgia
And in Florida, when it was hot

I bought it the night we arrived there
In a shop just along from Walgreens
It fitted me like a hand in a glove
And looked great with a Tee shirt and Jeans

Well I'm sure that it would've done anyway
But I never wore jeans come to that
It was tee shirt and shorts and sunscreen of course
And my now late lamented new hat

Me and that hat were like buddies
And I'm sure that you'd have to agree
Because I never went anywhere without taking him along
And he never went out without me

But I left it on the back seat of the Rental car
It was my fault, it has to be said
That's what you get for buying a Ten Dollar hat
And putting it on a Five Dollar head

The Heart Attack ...

So I'm sitting watching Telly. And I start to feeling rough
Could it be I've eat too much? or maybe not enough
Perhaps I'm dehydrated and I need something to drink
But then it all gets so much worse and I feel I start to sink

A tight grip deep inside my chest that spreads out down both arms
My visions getting blurry and I'm trying to stay calm
I'm feeling rather dizzy now and sweating like a horse
It doesn't take much working out a Heart Attack of course

Mary takes the telephone and dials 999
The paramedic 's at the door while She's still on the line
She's come prepared with gas and air to help me through the worst
The ambulance sounds blues and twos and through the door they burst

What happened next is just a blur, but that my heart stopped once was implied
I have to say, as fairgrounds go, it wasn't my favourite ride
But I won't hear a derogatory word, about the NHS
The treatment, care and compassion they gave was nothing but Simply the Best

So anyway I'm on the mend but I'll have to take things slow
But come on let's be honest, it's the only way I know
I'll soon be back to normal Fearless Brave and Bold
A Bus Pass and a Heart Attack? My God I'm getting old ...

Moonlight Serenade ...

It's 12.55 in the morning
and there's a snoring event in the ward
The bloke on my right has been going all night
in what I think is an E minor chord
Now the fella in bed number seven,
is snoring a great harmony
While the bass sound is played by old Farty pants
In the bed directly opposite me

There's a strange puffing sound from old Billy
In the bed that's just inside the door
The bloke in bed three has just gone for a wee,
or he just couldn't take anymore
From the next bed around, by the window,
is coming a strange hissing sound
It reminds me of something I heard in a funfair
Like an inflatable that's being let down

Now I'll enter a plea of not guilty,
I'm not joining in with this choir
At least not while aware but I really don't care,
when I drop off just what may transpire
Then the fella hooked up to the monitor,
let's out a baritone moan
Oh this is just too entertaining,
I'll sleep tomorrow ... when I get home. .

The Great British Caravan Holiday ...

The great British caravan holiday
As kids we all thought it was great
Getting the train down to Calcton or St. Osyth
The seaside ... We just couldn't wait

Getting a new pair of Wellington boots
And splashing in puddles for fun
Building a sancastle down on the beach
When the rain stopped and out came the sun

Walking along to the end of the pier
And watching the waves through the slats
Queuing to get on the Helter Skelter
And sitting on Coconut mats

Fish Paste or Spam in your sandwiches
Sand in your swimming costume
Sharing a bed with you Brother and Sister
With your Mum and Dad in the same room

Fish, Chips and Beans for your supper
A bucket and spade and a kite
Candy floss, Rock and a Handful of Pennies
To play the amusements at night

Falling asleep in the caravan
With the rain beating down on the roof
Midnight excursions to the shared toilet block
In pyjamas that weren't waterproof

Playing cards, Jigsaws and Orange squash
And Cup Cakes from a small plastic plate
The great British caravan holiday
As kids we all thought it was great

Improve With Age ...

I know that we've all noticed how, some things improve with age
A book that just gets better as you go from page to page
A fine wine takes the flavour from it's cask of solid oak
A pair of jeans that faded after leaving in to soak

There are, of course, some things that don't get better by the day
In fact if truth be told they even go the other way
Memory is one of them,.. and energy ..and joints
It seems like when it comes to us, Mother natures scoring points

Aches and pains, pulls and strains, a new one every day
Wrinkles where they weren't before, and hair that's turning Grey
I mean for other folks of course, this don't apply to me
Apart from the aches and pains and tiredness,
and of course there's memory

What do you mean, Not that again,
I said memory before?
How did you all get in my room?
and what's this typewriter for?
Did somebody mention some wine and a book
and getting on to the next page?
Now, where was I? Oh yeah, I know ...
Some things Improve with age

Sinatra Sings ...

I was stuck in traffic and was getting really stressed
I needed some relaxing music, So I reached for the best
The Chairman of the board I thought, Old Blue eyes is the Man
If anyone can calm me down then Frank Sinatra can

"The Shadow of you Smile" and now I'm starting to relax
"Let Me try Again", now this one really takes Me Back
Picking up the tempo "That's Life", My karaoke tune
I bet you know what's coming next, Yes "Fly Me to the Moon"

"Something Stupid", "Nice and Easy" then "Send in the Clowns"
Now my mood is lightening and my Temperatures coming down
I sing along to "September Song" and "It happened in Monterey"
Then the strings, and Frankie Sings, the anthem that's "My Way"

The traffic's all but disappeared, I'm almost home, It's fine
Time for one more song from Frank It's "I Will Drink The Wine"
Thank you Frank Sinatra, you saved my sanity
And as you often said "Oh No, They can't take that away from Me" .....

Southend ...

This week I'm being Grandad, as the children come to stay
The morning sun is shining bright and we're off out for the day
We head off down to Southend, the Cockney Cote D'Azur
For a walk along the beach to see the pier and so much more

It takes me back to childhood, and days out with our Mum
We'd come by train and set up camp, sometimes our Nan would come
Fish and Chips, a pickled onion, vinegar and salt
Candy Floss then feeling sick, it really wasn't our fault

The little ones still love it here, just like we always did
It still gives me a kick although it costs a nice few quid
The Kursal's now a Tesco, but at least it's not pulled down
The lights on the amusements spell, the names of different towns

New York New York and Monte Carlo, of course, Las Vegas Too
The biggest one is at the end.. "Electric Avenue"
But really at the heart of it, it's still the same old place
It puts a smile on any kid of any age's face

I think that it will always be, a favourite of mine
As faded glory seasides go, it really is still fine
Although when I was younger, it was all in Black And White
Ask me if I'd go again? ...
D'you know, I think I might

Cockney Air ...

I'm a Cockney, so they say,
East End Born and bred
I couldn't hear the Bells of Bow
but from Bow Road instead
We don't use cockney rhyming slang
like they did way back when
Except the odd time it slips out
and every now and then

The Cockney songs from yesteryear
come out once in a while
It's usually when we're Brahms and Liszt
and then they make me smile
"My old man said follow the van"
or "Show me the way to go home"
You've only gone to the local pub
not over Land or Sea or Foam

And even when we're far from home
in a strange way you feel kinda proud
To hear someone sing "On Muvver Kelly's Doorstep"
out of tune and a little too loud
So go up the Apples and Brush your 'Ampsteads
and comb your Barnet Fair
And go outside and take some deep breaths
of our famous Cockney air ....

The Storm ...

The Boats are all moored in safe harbour
The Fishermen tucked up in their beds
A storm is brewing, just off the coast
And coming inland off the head

The waves are now building, the birds have all flown
The rain's started lashing the shore
The lighthouse stands silent, long since abandoned
The light doesn't flash anymore

The wind buffers windows and doors on the seafront
A car alarm screams in the night
The streets of the town are now running like rivers
The drains cannot cope with its might

The noise of the Thunder, the Flash of the Lightening
A bedraggled dog cowers in fright
All natures dark forces are visited on us
On this cold and dark winters night

But then as the storm starts to ease and relent
And the dawn breaks way out to the east
The rain slows to nothing the tide has receded
The sea wall defences not breached

Rubbish is strewn all over wet streets
The Place has been tipped upside down
The clean up begins as nobody wins
The Winter's not kind to this town

Absent Friends ...

There is a school reunion soon which I can not attend
I have made arrangements and I'm busy that weekend
But those of you who know me won't be surprised at all
I never turned up half the time when we were back at school

A lot of things have happened to us with the passing years
Most of us lost touch with who we used to call our peers
The girls have turned to women and the boys grown into men
No-one warned us we'd get old, can't we try again ?

And now we all have Facebook and our St Paul's Way School page
Where we log on to see how much we've all improved with age
We share our mem'ries, post our pictures and we reminisce
On days gone by, when we were young and times that we all miss

I hope that this reunion is the greatest one of all
The years roll back and you post lots of pictures on our wall
But tag their faces, when you post so ev'ryone can see
And raise a glass to absent friends, 'cause one of them is me

My Bestest Girl and Me...

We've bought a bit of Gala Pie and Salad for our tea
A nice traditional summer Sunday, Like it used to be
The only bit we're leaving out, is the Sunday Roast
With no Grandchildren, just us two, we're going down the coast

I think we'll head to Whitstable, or at least that's where we'll start
And just as long as nature and the weather play their part
We'll have a stroll and rest a while, and sit and watch the sea
And maybe have an Ice Cream, just my bestest girl and Me

So I'll Slap a bit of sunscreen on, in case I burn my head
Tee Shirt, shorts and Flip Flops, or perhaps my Crocs instead
We'll park the car and walk as far, and back as suits our mood
At least down to the market where they sell the fresh seafood

Then right back to the start and Gala Pie for Sunday tea
And maybe have an early night we'll have to wait and see
So, have a lovely day but take it easy 'cos you see
We're going to the Seaside, My bestest girl and Me

Near a River ...

Near a river called the Thames, where it twists and turns and bends
and nearly ties itself into a bow
Is the part of London town where my roots were first laid down
and the basis of most everything I know
East End boys, no airs and graces, scuffed up shoes with busted laces,
playing in the street from dawn 'til night
Penny up the wall and stone raids, Hot bread pudding that your Nan made,
when Paraffin was used for heat and light

The East End was a place of joy, back when I was just a boy
from Mile End Road to Poplar and beyond
From Stratford down to Stepney, and from Vicky Park to Hackney,
we always new the place where we belonged
Six of chips and sherbet pips, Marbles, Gobs and Seaside trips,
Run-outs, Knock down Ginger and a kite
A pub on every corner and a Copper who would warn ya!
If he thought that you were out too late at night

The TV was in monochrome and next to no one had a phone,
we went around and knocked on our mates doors
Is Johnny coming out to play? No he's not now go away,
He'd be out later and he'd come round yours
Back then we had the docks of course and the Milkman had a Cart and Horse,
we had Pie and Mash or Saveloy for tea
They say that we were poor back then but looking back on it again
I have to say it's difficult to see

London is as London does, I love the East End most because
That's the place my heart will ever go
Near a river called the Thames, where it twists and turns and bends
and nearly ties itself into a bow

200

Sunshiney Day ...

What are we going to do with ourselves
On this beautiful sunshiney day?,
Unless of course sunshiney isn't a word
Well I've written it now anyway

Yesterday was spent, on the North coast of Kent
And now that this Sunday's arrived
The car has been through a lot this week
So I might leave it there on the drive

The grass needs a cut and the front gate won't shut
So I may do a few jobs 'round here
Mary could lay in the sun for the day
With a sandwich for lunch and a Beer

I won't wait for the showers, I'll water the flowers
And dead head the ones that are dead
But don't get me wrong, that won't take very long
Then I'll get my deckchair from the shed

It's one of those days when we're just gonna laze
And we're not going down to the coast
But before we get started, I'm having the largest
Cup of tea and two slices of toast

Housework ...

You know when you're doing the housework
And you decide to move the armchair
You've hoovered around it for a couple of weeks
And you wonder what lives under there

Now it's not like we're having visitors
Or that anyones coming to stay
It's just that while flicking the duster around
I got a bit carried away

So anyway, out came the armchair
And the sofa and then the T.V.
A couple of Malteezers, various loom bands
A King of Hearts and 50p

A couple of old triple A batteries
A rubber hair band and a Smurf
A Silver ring out of a Christmas Cracker
I wonder just how much that's worth

You know when you're doing the housework
And you decide to move the armchair
Well I've just done that but I needn't have bothered
'cos no one else knew what was there ...lol

The Only Way Is ...

They tell me the only way is Essex
So I thought I'd come up here and see
I'm drinking my coffee in Costa in Lakeside
About two hundred strangers and me

There's one bloke with tattoos all over his face
To be honest I'm a little bit scared
I guess that I must have been staring at him
Because he just looked over and glared

I've never seen so many iPhones
In so many colours and hues
And small caramel Machiatos
And a Barista who looks like Tom Cruise

There's a girl over there, with lovely blue hair
She's in her pyjamas I think
And surely her shoes must be slippers
They're all kind of fluffy and pink

The kids are all dressed in designer attire
It's like all their birthdays have come
And one little cutie who's doing her duty
Dressed exactly the same as her Mum

They say that the only way is Essex
Well it certainly starts with an E
I think I've found out what it's the only way to
It's back to the East End for Me

I Still Remember ...

I still remember all the teacher's names from back at school
And how I laughed at Norman Wisdom when he played the fool
The '66 Cup Final and when Geoff Hurst scored the winner
The problem is I don't remember, what I had for yesterday's dinner

I still remember every word to "I wanna hold your hand"
Day trips down to Southend beach, building castles in the sand
That holiday to Austria when I rented yellow skis
The problem is I don't remember where I've put my keys

I still remember my first wages, Four pounds Ten a week
The first time that I ever heard a shop called a boutique
The first time that my Mum gave me a key to our front door
The problem is I don't know what I just went upstairs for

It goes to show my memory's good, there's nothing wrong at all
If I remember all those things from when I was only small
I still remember all the words I learned in Spanish classes
Give me a second, I'll read them to you,
now where did I put my glasses ....

Life in the Bus Lane ...

I got me a bus pass from Boris
So I travel for free around town
I can go on the Docklands Light Railway
Or the bus or the whole Underground

I got it because I turned Sixty
And they figured that I'd paid enough
But the truth is I never really used it before
I have my own car for that stuff

But here I am, on Public transport
And the City does seem kind of strange
I can go anywhere without ever a care
About parking or having the right change

Now the Rush hour, just trust me that's mental
You don't want to go out in that
But the fun there can be, between 10 and say 3
Beats driving into a cocked hat

The buskers who play in the underground
The driverless DLR trains
The traffic lights, road works and diverted traffic
The buses treat all with disdain

We've traveled all over, my Oyster and me
Underground Overground Wombling free
But it's home for a nap now, I'm feeling quite tired
Life in the Bus lane. .. Thank God I'm retired. ..

The Barbecue ...

The smell of burning rocket fuel
Wafting out over the sea
There's a little old bloke, getting covered in smoke
And that little old bloke is me

Yep, somebody's lit up their barbecue
And unfortunately we're being choked
I feel like I know what a kipper feels like
When the poor little sod's being smoked

I think that the best thing to do is to move
'Cos obviously I'm in the way
The least they could do is offer me a sausage
I smell like one now anyway

But bless 'em, they're having a lovely day out
As they picnic out here in the sun
I think they should take those burgers off though
By the smell of things I think that they're done

Cilla ...

"What's it all about ?" she sung,
we ask that question now
Anyone who had a heart
is saddened at this hour
We all felt like we knew her,
she was our own Superstar
Cilla Black, we'll miss you
and we'll miss your repertoire

"Oh you are a mucky kid",
reminds us of the things we did
"Love of the Loved" and "It's for you",
"Step inside Love" and "Alfie" too
"You're my World"
was a favourite of mine
And "Baby it's You",
just to make the thing rhyme

The Red haired girl from Liverpool
who never lost her style
Sung songs to tear your heartstrings,
and songs to make you smile
She never lost her accent
and for that we all loved her
And somehow, Care and There and Fair
all somehow rhymed with Fur

Gone too soon, as many do,
no time for long goodbyes
A light's gone out, She's left the building,
no more Surprise Surprise
We'll play your records now
and when we feel the time is right
Go now on your last Blind Date,
God Bless, God speed, Goodnight ...xx

London by Night ...

London by night is a sight to behold
The brand new and shiny alongside the old
All dressed up in argon and neon ablaze
In colours to rival the very sun's rays

The rich and the poor join the throng of the street
The native and tourist become it's heartbeat
From the seemier side that still dwells in Soho
To the Palace, to Big Ben, to a Theatreland show

A walk by the river with twinkling lights
The buildings in Docklands that reach dizzy heights
St. Paul's Cathedral with it's huge floodlit dome
The shadowy tower the ravens call home

The Thames threads a ribbon of life through the town
With bridges traversing it all the way down
From Putney to Dartford and all in between
The river boats pass underneath them, unseen

A beautiful city, I'm sure you'd all say
It's treasures are plenty in the cold light of day
When lighted it glitters like silver and gold
London by night is a sight to behold.

At Home ...

I wish I was at home right now
With the central heating on
Feet up watching television,
There where I belong

My wife there sitting in her chair
A nice long glass of red
The Little ones both Gently snoring,
Tucked up in their bed

I wish I was at home right now
Chilled in my Calvin Klein's
And Marvel Super Hero shirt
I bought myself on line

The beauty of these wishes is
That they have all come true
I have all I could wish for
And I hope that you have too .....

Raining ...

What a lousy day today
It was raining dogs and cats
People carrying big umbrellas
Others wearing big hats

Hurrying, scurrying ducking inside
Jumping on buses for a fifty yard ride
Everyone's wet, soaked through to the skin
Carrying bags with their wet shopping in

But come on it's England and I know that it's summer
And sometimes the weather's a bit of a bummer
But through June and July, the sun shone every day
We'll most of the days it did anyway

You can't have a rainbow without the rain
And the rain in Spain stays mainly on the plain
And it's good for the garden and blah blah blah blah
Take my advice just stay in where you are. ..

Be Nice ...

I read a thing on Facebook
that has stayed with me since then
I don't know if you saw it
but I'll post it here again
It seemed to me to sum up
all the things we share in life
So much so I read it out
and shared it with my Wife

It touched me so and now I know
to try to do what's right
And when I don't my Wife reminds me
of what we read that night
It is a very simple tenet
and it also can be fun
"The world is full of nice people,
If you can't find one Be one"

Bed Time ...

I'm gonna go to bed soon,
I can hardly stay awake
But I don't want to go to early,
that could be a big mistake
The earlier I go to bed at night,
the more times I get up
This never happened years ago
when I was a young pup

I wake up at the slightest noise
and wonder, Should I go?
It's cold out there and warm in here,
this time the answer's no
I close my eyes and climb aboard
the night time carousel
I'll just go back to sleep again
but wait, Oh flippin' hell...

Alright then quickly to the bathroom
and straight back into bed
Don't turn on the bedside lamp
use your night vision instead
And as I go, I stub my toe
and shout something beginning with F
Thank God that when the wife's asleep
she goes a little deaf

I think I might have broke my toe
but soon go back to sleep
When I wake again I've got
my blankets in a heap
I'm flippin' freezing now and once again I need to go
I wish I'd stayed up longer...
you'd think by know I'd know

GNGB ...

Another day is over
and another race is run
Another night is on us
and another tale is spun
Another way for us to say
we faced another test
And passed with flying colours
just by giving of our best

But now it's time for Hypnos
who will take us into sleep
And pray your God will bless you
and your sleeping soul will keep..
..in safety, for the morning comes
more quickly than we know
And then we must be bushy tailed
and ready for the show

So sleep the sleep of innocents
and dream as dreamers do
For that's the time the world will rhyme
and energy renew
Sleep well my friends as this day ends
and keep it safe and warm
Alone or in pairs as you climb the stairs,
and let consciousness transform

Goodnight God Bless ...

Printed in October 2021
by Rotomail Italia S.p.A., Vignate (MI) - Italy